PRENTICE HALL
SCIENCE

Activity Book

MATTER

Building Block of the Universe

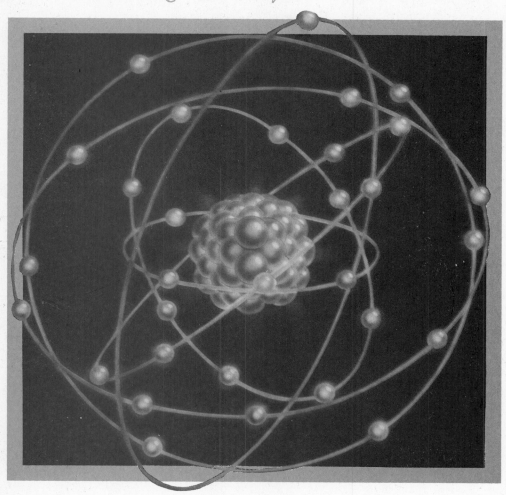

Prentice Hall
Englewood Cliffs, New Jersey
Needham, Massachusetts

Activity Book

PRENTICE HALL SCIENCE
Matter
Building Block of the Universe

ISBN 0-13-986969-7

2 3 4 5 6 7 8 9 10   96 95 94 93 92

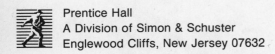

Prentice Hall
A Division of Simon & Schuster
Englewood Cliffs, New Jersey 07632

Contents

To the Teacher

The materials in the *Activity Book* are designed to assist you in teaching the *Prentice Hall Science* program. These materials will be especially helpful to you in accommodating a wide range of student ability levels. In particular, the activities have been designed to reinforce and extend a variety of science skills and to encourage critical thinking, problem solving, and discovery learning. The highly visual format of many activities heightens student interest and enthusiasm.

All the materials in the *Activity Book* have been developed to facilitate student comprehension of, and interest in, science. Pages intended for student use may be made into overhead transparencies and masters or used as photocopy originals. The reproducible format allows you to have these items easily available in the quantity you need. All appropriate answers to questions and activities are found at the end of each section in a convenient Answer Key.

CHAPTER MATERIALS

In order to stimulate and increase student interest, the *Activity Book* includes a wide variety of activities and worksheets. All the activities and worksheets are correlated to individual chapters in the student textbook.

Table of Contents

Each set of chapter materials begins with a Table of Contents that lists every component for the chapter and the page number on which it begins. The Table of Contents also lists the number of the page on which the Answer Key for the chapter activities and worksheets begins. In addition, the Table of Contents page for each chapter has a shaded bar running along the edge of the page. This shading will enable you to easily spot where a new set of chapter materials begins.

Whenever an activity might be considered a problem-solving or discovery-learning activity, it is so marked on the Contents page. In addition, each activity that can be used for cooperative-learning groups has an asterisk beside it on the Contents page.

First in the chapter materials is a Chapter Discovery. The Chapter Discovery is best used prior to students reading the chapter. It will enable students to discover for themselves some of the scientific concepts discussed within the chapter. Because of their highly visual design, simplicity, and hands-on approach to discovery learning, the Discovery Activities are particularly appropriate for ESL students in a cooperative-learning setting.

Chapter Activities

Chapter activities are especially visual, often asking students to draw conclusions from diagrams, graphs, tables, and other forms of data. Many chapter activities enable the student to employ problem-solving and critical-thinking skills. Others allow the student to utilize a discovery-learning approach to the topics covered in the chapter. In addition, most chapter activities are appropriate for cooperative-learning groups.

Laboratory Investigation Worksheet

Each chapter of the textbook contains a full-page Laboratory Investigation. A Laboratory Investigation worksheet in each set of chapter materials repeats the textbook Laboratory Investigation and provides formatted space for writing observations and conclusions. Students are aided by a formatted worksheet, and teachers can easily evaluate and grade students' results and progress. Answers to the Laboratory Investigation are provided in the Answer Key following the chapter materials, as well as in the Annotated Teacher's Edition of the textbook.

Answer Key

At the end of each set of chapter materials is an Answer Key for all activities and worksheets in the chapter.

SCIENCE READING SKILLS

Each textbook in *Prentice Hall Science* ends with a special feature called the Science Gazette. Each gazette contains three articles.

The first article in every Science Gazette—called Adventures in Science— describes a particular discovery, innovation, or field of research of a scientist or group of scientists. Some of the scientists profiled in Adventures in Science are well known; others are not yet famous but have made significant contributions to the world of science. These articles provide students with firsthand knowledge about how scientists work and think, and give some insight into the scientists' personal lives as well.

Issues in Science is the second article in every gazette. This article provides a nonbiased description of a specific area of science in which various members of the scientific community or the population at large hold diverging opinions. Issues in Science articles introduce students to some of the "controversies" raging in science at the present time. While many of these issues are debated strictly in scientific terms, others involve social issues that pertain to science as well.

The third article in every Science Gazette is called Futures in Science. The setting of each Futures in Science article is some 15 to 150 years in the future and describes some of the advances people may encounter as science progresses through the years. However, these articles cannot be considered "science fiction," as they are all extrapolations of current scientific research.

The Science Gazette articles can be powerful motivators in developing an interest in science. However, they have been written with a second purpose in mind. These articles can be used as science readers. As such, they will both reinforce and enrich your students' ability to read scientific material. In order to better assess the science reading skills of your students, this *Activity Book* contains a variety of science reading activities based on the gazette articles. Each gazette article has an activity that can be distributed to students in order to evaluate their science reading skills.

There are a variety of science reading skills included in this *Activity Book*. These skills include Finding the Main Idea, Previewing, Critical Reading, Making Predictions, Outlining, Using Context Clues, and Making Inferences. These basic study skills are essential in understanding the content of all subject matter, and they can be particularly useful in the comprehension of science materials. Mastering such study skills can help students to study, learn new vocabulary terms, and understand information found in their textbooks.

Contents

CHAPTER 1 ■ General Properties of Matter

*Appropriate for cooperative learning

Discovering Properties of Matter

Everything shown on these pages is made of matter. Observe each picture carefully, then answer the questions.

marble   **baseball**   **bowling ball**

1. How are these objects different from one another? _____

_____

_____

How are they similar? _____

_____

_____

Ping-Pong **Wood** **Steel**

2. Tell how these objects are alike, and how they are different. _____

_____

_____

Suppose the objects were placed in water. What do you think would happen? _____

_____

_____

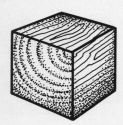
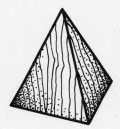
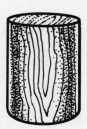

3. All of these objects are made of wood. How are they alike? _____

_____

_____

How are they different? _____

_____

A   B   C

4. Describe the matter that fills each container. _____

_____

_____

Which of the three containers could hold the contents of the other two? _____

A   B

5. Describe the matter in balloon A. What is this substance doing to the balloon? _____

_____

_____

How is balloon B different from balloon A? What must be true about the matter

inside balloon B? _____

_____

_____

6. Tell how these objects are alike, and how they are different. _____

_____

_____

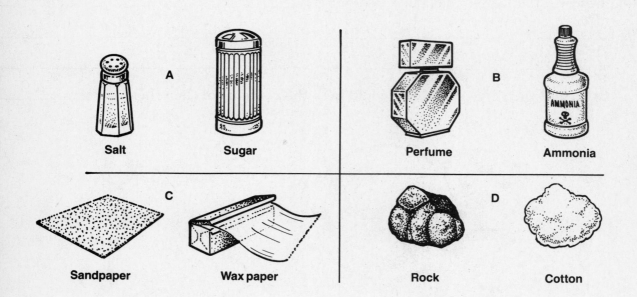

A Salt   Sugar

B Perfume   Ammonia

C Sandpaper   Wax paper

D Rock   Cotton

7. Suppose that you were blindfolded. How could you tell the items in each pair apart?

a. _____

b. _____

c. _____

d. _____

8. Which object contains more matter? _____

Suppose each object were allowed to roll down the hill. Which do you think would

be harder to stop? _____

_____

Critical Thinking and Application

9. Based on your answers to questions 1 through 8, what do you think are some

characteristics of all types of matter? _____

_____

_____

_____

What are some characteristics that seem to be different for different types of

matter? _____

_____

_____

_____

_____

_____

Activity

Quick Weight Changes

Use the information about the gravity on each of the following planets and the moon to predict the weight of the girl.

Earth = 1
Jupiter = 2.7
Pluto = 0.4
Moon = 0.16
Saturn = 1.2

Earth

_____440_____ newtons

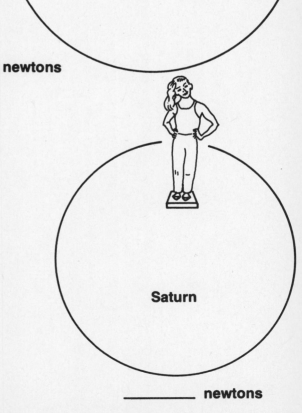

Jupiter

_____ newtons

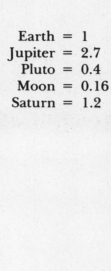

Moon   **Pluto**

_____ newtons   _____ newtons

Saturn

_____ newtons

Name _____ Class _____ Date _____

Density Drill

Some objects tend to be "heavy," while other objects seem "light." But unless you are comparing the same volume of each object, these descriptions have little value. And that is where the concept of density comes in. Density refers to how much mass an object has in a particular volume. Scientifically, density is described as mass per unit volume, or density = mass/volume. Because mass is measured in grams, and volume is measured in cubic centimeters, the unit for density is grams per cubic centimeter.

If the mass and volume of an object are known, its density can be determined by dividing the volume value into the mass value. Similarly, if the density and mass are known, the object's volume can be determined by dividing the density value into the mass value. Finally, if an object's density and volume are known, its mass can be found by multiplying these two values. You can see how density, mass, and volume are related by doing this activity. In each situation, you are given enough information to determine the unknown value in the formula D = M/V.

A. 1. The mass of object A, as shown by the positions of the balance riders, is _____ g.

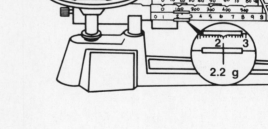

2. The volume of object A, as indicated by the given dimensions, is _____ cm³.

3. Using the formula $D = \dfrac{M}{V}$, calculate the density of object A. _____ g/cm³

4. If object A is cut into two equal parts, what is the density of one half of A? _____ g/cm³ Of the other half? _____ g/cm³. How does the density of object A compare to the density of half of object A? _____

B. 1. The mass of object B has been determined to be 125 gs.

2. The volume of object B, as indicated by the change in fluid level in the cylinder, is _____ .

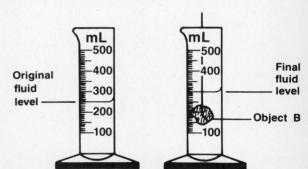

3. Using the formula $D = \dfrac{M}{V}$, calculate the density of object B.

_____ g/cm^3

C. 1. Object C is a perfect cube. The mass of object C, as shown by the position of the balance riders, is

_____ g.

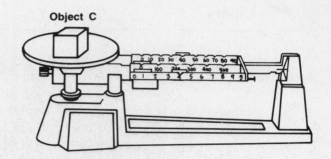
Object C

2. The density of object C has been determined to be 5.5 g/cm^3.

3. Using the formula $V = \dfrac{M}{D}$, calculate the volume of object C. _____ cm^3

4. Since object C is a perfect cube, determine the length of each side of that cube. _Hint:_ The formula for the volume of a cube is $V = L \times W \times H$. Length of any side of cube C = _____ cm.

D. 1. The density of object D has been determined to be 1.4 g/cm^3.

2. The volume of object D, as indicated by the change in fluid level in the cylinder, is

_____ cm^3.

3. Using the formula $M = D \times V$, calculate the mass of object D.

_____ g

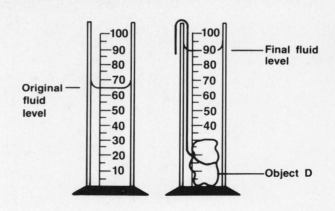

Activity

General Properties of Matter

Does It Float?

The density of water is 1 gram per milliliter, 1 g/mL. If an object has a density less than 1 g/mL, it will float in water. If the object's density is greater than 1 g/mL, it will sink.

In this activity you will estimate the volume and the mass of several objects. Then you will use the density formula, Density = Mass/Volume, to get an approximate value for the density of the object. Finally, you will predict if the object will float.

One way to estimate the volume of an object like a comb is to imagine its shape as approximating a regular geometric shape, such as a small rectangular box.

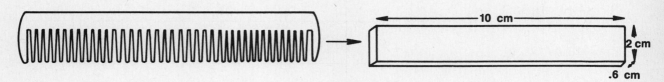

$$\text{Volume} = 10 \text{ cm} \times 2 \text{ cm} \times .6 \text{ cm}$$
$$= 12 \text{ cm}^3$$
$$= 12 \text{ mL}$$

You will have to subtract about one-third of the volume to take into account the spaces between the teeth of the comb.

⅓ × 12 mL = 4 mL, so 12 mL − 4 mL = 8 mL = Total volume

Description	Estimated Mass	Estimated Volume	Approximate Density	Does It Float?
Nylon comb	10 g	8 mL	10 g/8 mL = 1.25 g/cm^3	no
9-volt calculator battery				
Aluminum foil ball				
Pencil				
Large ice cube				
Small ice cube				
Softball				
Rubik's cube (small version)				
Apple				

Activity

General Properties of Matter

Volume—Taking Up Space

Matter is anything that has mass and volume. Volume is the amount of space an object takes up. But, did you know that within the object itself there are empty spaces? Although liquids and solids appear to be smooth and continuous, there are spaces between the individual particles making up the matter. You can demonstrate this fact by gathering the following materials and doing the steps listed. You will be making a model that shows how particles of matter are arranged. You may be surprised by the results.

To do this activity, you will need four graduated cylinders, isopropyl alcohol (rubbing alcohol), water, marbles, and some sand.

1. Measure exactly 50.0 mL of water in one cylinder and 50.0 mL of alcohol in another. **CAUTION:** *Keep isopropyl alcohol away from flames.*

2. Predict the total volume if the contents of the two cylinders are combined. Now combine the contents into one cylinder and read the resulting volume. Is it what you expected? Can you explain what has happened?

_____

_____

_____

3. Fill another graduated cylinder to the 50.0 mL mark with marbles. Fill the remaining cylinder with 50.0 mL of sand.

4. Combine the contents of these two cylinders and note the final volume.

_____

_____

_____

5. Explain your results. How do these results provide a model for the way particles are arranged in matter?

_____

_____

_____

_____

Laboratory Investigation

Inertia

Problem
How does an object's mass affect its inertia?

Materials *(per group)*
several shoe boxes
objects of various masses to fit in the shoe boxes
smooth table top
household broom
meterstick or metric ruler

Procedure
1. Place an object in each shoe box and replace the lid on the shoe box. Number each box. (Your teacher may provide you with several shoe boxes that are already prepared.)
2. Position the box so that it hangs over the edge of the table by 8 cm.
3. Stand the broom directly behind the table. Put your foot on the straw part of the broom to hold it in place.
4. Slowly move the broom handle back away from the box.
5. When you release the handle, the broomstick should spring forward, striking the middle of the end of the box.
6. Measure how far the box moves across the table after it is struck by the broom.
7. Repeat this procedure with each of the boxes. Try to use the same force each time.

Observations
1. Enter the box number and the distance moved in a chart similar to the one shown here.

Box Number	Distance Traveled

2. Open the boxes and examine the contents. Record what object was in each box.

_____

_____

_____

Analysis and Conclusions

1. What part of the definition of inertia applies to your observations about the movements of the boxes? _____

_____

2. Why do you think some boxes moved farther than others? _____

_____

3. What do you notice about the objects that moved farthest from the resting position? What do you notice about the objects that moved the shortest distance from the resting position? _____

_____

4. Why was it important that you used the same force each time a box was struck?

_____

_____

5. **On Your Own** You can compare the masses of different objects by using a balance. Can you propose another way to determine the masses of different objects?

_____

_____

Answer Key

Chapter Discovery: Discovering Properties of Matter

1. They are different sizes. They are all round and hard; all are used to play games or sports. **2.** They are the same size and shape. They are made of different materials. The Ping-Pong ball and wooden ball would float; the steel ball would sink. **3.** Possible answers might include: some properties of wood; the fact that these blocks might be used to build things; or just hard, smooth, and so forth. They are different shapes. **4.** Possible answers include: liquid; white; nourishing as a food; tastes creamy and a little bit sweet. Container C. **5.** Properties of air include: colorless, gas, very light, and so on. It is making the balloon get larger. Balloon B can float in air. Matter in balloon B must be lighter (less dense) than air. **6.** All are fruit or vegetables that can be eaten; all are about the same size; differences include color, taste, shape, and texture. **7.** a. Taste each item for saltiness and sweetness. b. Smell each item. c. Touch each item for roughness and smoothness. d. Hold each item for hardness and softness and weight. **8.** Wagon B. Wagon B. **9.** Accept all reasonable answers. Some students may realize that all matter has mass and weight and takes up space. They may also observe that matter can exist as solids, liquids, and gases. Students should recognize shape, hardness, density, weight, color, odor, taste, texture, size, and phase.

Problem-Solving Activity: Quick Weight Changes

Jupiter = 1188; Moon = 70.4; Pluto = 176; Saturn = 528.

Problem-Solving Activity: Density Drill

Object A 1. 152.2 **2.** 18 **3.** 8.46 **4.** 8.46, 8.46 It is the same. Density is not affected by size or shape. **Object B 2.** 50 mL (50 cm³) **3.** 2.5 **Object C 1.** 44 **3.** 8 **4.** 2 **Object D 2.** 25 **3.** 35

Discovery Activity: Does It Float?

9-volt calculator battery 40.9 g, 4.5 cm × 1.6 cm × 2.5 cm = 18 cm³, 40.9 g/18 cm³ = 2.27 g/cm³, no **Aluminum foil ball** 90.4 g, answers will vary, density = 2.7 g/cm³, no **Pencil** 3.8 g, V = $\pi r^2 h$ = 10.9 cm³, 0.35 g/cm³, yes **Large ice cube** Answers will vary, density = 0.92 g/cm³, yes **Small ice cube** Answers will vary but density is the same as the large ice cube, yes **Softball** 100 g will vary, 113 cm³, 0.88 g/cm³, yes **Rubik's cube** 24.5 g, 3 cm on a side = 27 cm³, 0.9 g/cm³, yes **Apple** Answers will vary, density = 0.88 g/cm³, yes

Discovery Activity: Volume—Taking Up Space

2. Predictions will vary, but most students will predict that the resulting volume will be 100 mL. The volume of the two liquids will be less than 100 mL. Students may have difficulty explaining their observations. You may want them to wait until after they have mixed the sand and marbles together to explain what happens when they mix water and alcohol. **4.** When the sand and marbles are mixed, the result is less than 100 mL. Some of the sand flows into the spaces between the marbles. **5.** Students can infer that there are spaces between molecules in the two liquids. These spaces are filled when the liquids are mixed. The final volume is less than the volume of the two liquids before they are mixed.

Laboratory Investigation: Inertia

Observations 1.–2. Students' chart entries should accurately reflect the data they collected during the investigation. Students should note that the stronger the initial force, the longer the distance the box traveled. **Analysis and Conclusions 1.** An object's mass causes it to resist changes in motion, or to exhibit inertia. **2.–3.** The boxes that contained more mass had greater inertia and were not set in as rapid a motion as were the lighter boxes.   **4.** If the force does not remain a constant, then there would be two different variables in the experiment, and it would not be clear if the results were due to inertia or to differing forces.

5. Students' suggestions should show that they understand the difference between mass and weight. One possibility is to use one object as a standard, then perform inertia tests on it and on other objects, and assign mass values on this basis.

Contents

*Appropriate for cooperative learning

Chapter Discovery   **Physical and Chemical Changes**

Observing Changes in Matter

Materials
4 sugar cubes
glass of water
spoon
mortar and pestle
Bunsen burner
test tube
tongs

Procedure
Part A

1. Pick up one of the sugar cubes and observe it carefully. Describe the sugar cube in terms of the following properties:

    a. Size _____

    b. Shape _____

    c. Color _____

    d. Taste _____

    e. Hardness _____

    f. Texture _____

2. Take two sugar cubes and use the mortar and pestle to crush them into a powder.

3. Observe the powder. How have you changed the sugar?

    _____

    _____

    In what ways has the sugar not been changed?

    _____

4. Take the crushed sugar and pour it into the glass of water. Stir with the spoon.

5. Look carefully at the mixture. Is the sugar still visible? How has the sugar changed?

_____

_____

_____

_____

6. Take a taste of the water. Is the sugar still present? How can you tell?

_____

7. Suppose you could not taste the water. Can you think of any other way to prove that the sugar is still present?

_____

_____

Part B

1. Take two sugar cubes and place them in the test tube.

2. Light the Bunsen burner. **CAUTION:** _Be very careful when lighting and using a Bunsen burner._ Using the tongs to hold the test tube, heat the test tube until the sugar burns. Observe the contents of the test tube carefully as you heat it.

3. What do you see happening? Look closely at the sides and mouth of the tube as well as in the bottom. Do you see any substances forming in the tube that were not in the tube when you started?

_____

_____

_____

_____

4. Remove the test tube from the heat and let it cool. Turn off the Bunsen burner.

5. Observe the contents of the test tube. Describe the substance in the bottom of the tube in terms of the following properties:

a. Size _____

_____

b. Shape _____

c. Color _____

d. Taste (**CAUTION:** *Do not swallow the substance.*)

_____

e. Hardness _____

f. Texture _____

6. Recall the two sugar cubes that you started with. How has the sugar changed?

_____

_____

_____

7. Is the sugar still present in the test tube? How can you tell?

_____

_____

_____

_____

Critical Thinking and Application

8. Compare the changes in the sugar that took place in Part A with the changes that took place in Part B. How are these changes different?

_____

_____

_____

9. The changes that took place in Part A are called physical changes, while the changes that took place in Part B are called chemical changes. Based on your observations, how would you define a physical change? How would you define a chemical change?

_____

_____

_____

_____

**ctivity**

Physical and Chemical Changes

Observing a Phase Change

Carefully heat a pan of water until the water boils. Then, using tongs, lower a drinking glass, open end down, over the boiling water. **CAUTION:** *Exercise care when working with heated objects and glassware.* Describe the changes you see. How would you explain these changes?

_____

_____

_____

_____

_____

In the space below, draw diagrams of the changes.

Activity

Physical and Chemical Changes

Properties of Matter

Physical and Chemical Changes

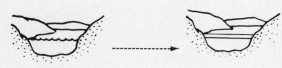

Type of Change

1. _____

2. _____

3. _____

4. _____

Phase Changes

Type of Physical Change	Change in Molecular Movement
5. _____	_____
6. _____	_____
7. _____	_____
8. _____	_____

ctivity

Physical and Chemical Changes

General and Specific Properties

1. Collect at least six different kinds of objects as samples of matter. You might include rocks, pieces of wood or glass, and objects made by people.

2. Describe each sample by listing some of its properties.

3. List the general properties that you used to tell that the sample was matter.

4. List the specific properties, such as color, shape, and hardness, that you used to identify each sample. These specific properties are those that enabled you to tell the samples apart.

5. After you have completed your descriptions, give them to a classmate and see if he or she can identify each object or kind of matter from the properties you listed.

Sample 1 _____

General
Properties _____
_____

Specific
Properties _____
_____
_____

Sample 2 _____

General
Properties _____
_____

Specific
Properties _____
_____
_____

Sample 3 _____

General
Properties _____
_____

Specific
Properties _____
_____
_____

Sample 4 _____

General
Properties _____
_____

Specific
Properties _____
_____
_____

Sample 5 _____

General
Properties _____
_____

Specific
Properties _____
_____
_____

Sample 6 _____

General
Properties _____
_____

Specific
Properties _____
_____
_____

Activity

Identifying Physical and Chemical Changes

Identifying physical and chemical changes is an important science skill. Table A provides several examples of situations in which a substance undergoes a change. Decide if the description indicates a physical or a chemical change. Write your answer in the appropriate box. Also, briefly state why you made your choice. Table B provides several substances that can undergo both physical and chemical changes. In the appropriate box, describe what could be done to the substances to bring about these changes.

Table A

	Type of Change	Reason for Choice
1. While you are filling the gas tank on your minibike, a small amount of gasoline spills but soon disappears.		
2. As the minibike runs, less gasoline remains in the gas tank as carbon dioxide leaves the exhaust.		
3. After swimming in the ocean and resting on the beach, you are no longer wet, but your skin has a salty film on it.		
4. After stirring the sugar you added to some iced tea, the sugar disappears but the tea tastes sweet.		

Table B

	Description of a Physical Change That Could Happen	Description of a Chemical Change That Could Happen
1. Raw egg		
2. Pencil		
3. Antacid tablet		
4. Green plant		
5. Bicycle frame		

Activity

Physical and Chemical Changes

Phase Changes

The accompanying graph shows the relationship between temperature and heat energy during the phase changes of water. Study the graph and answer the questions.

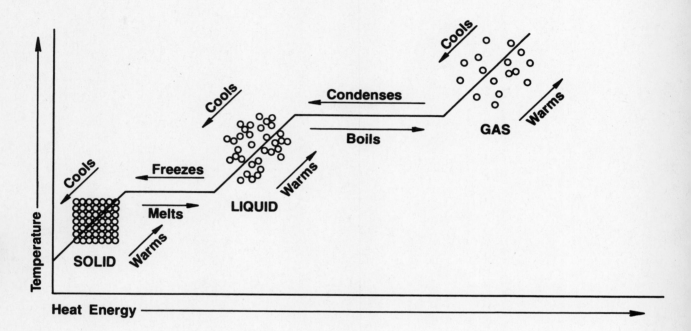

1. Does the temperature increase during melting? _____

2. Is energy required for each phase change? _____

3. Can both liquid water and steam exist at 100°C? _____

4. What must be changed, temperature or heat energy, during

   condensation? _____

5. How would you describe the change in the arrangement of particles as heat energy

   and temperature increase? _____

6. What rule can you state about the relationship between phase changes and

   temperature? Between phase changes and heat energy? _____

   _____

Activity

Pouring a Gas

Carbon dioxide is a colorless, odorless gas that does not support burning. You can easily make carbon dioxide by mixing vinegar and baking soda. Although you cannot see the carbon dioxide, you can prove it is present and it can be poured by doing the following activity.

1. Light a small candle and use some of the wax from it to make the candle stand upright in a small dish. **CAUTION:** *Be very careful when working with matches and a lighted candle.*

2. Pour some vinegar into a glass. Then drop a small amount of baking soda into the vinegar. Notice what happens. What kind of change is this? _____

3. Now slowly tip the glass over the candle flame as if you were pouring something on the flame. Do not let any of the liquid pour onto the flame. What happens to the flame? Why?

_____

_____

_____

Activity _____ **Physical and Chemical Changes**

Behavior of Gases

Using Boyle's law and Charles's law, fill in the blanks in each of the pairs of diagrams. Do not be concerned with the absence of units on the number values. Use the numbers only to help you determine relationships between volume, pressure, and temperature.

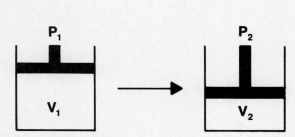

$P_1 = 10$
$V_1 = 100$

$P_2 = 20$
$V_2 =$ _____

1. _____ law

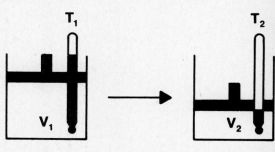

$T_1 = 40$
$V_1 = 120$

$T_2 = 10$
$V_2 =$ _____

4. _____ law

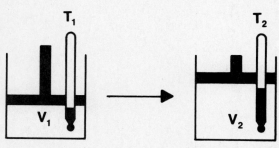

$T_1 = 15$
$V_1 = 70$

$T_2 = 30$
$V_2 =$ _____

2. _____ law

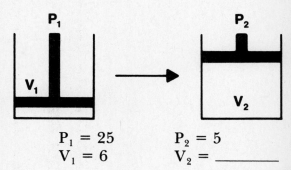

$P_1 = 25$
$V_1 = 6$

$P_2 = 5$
$V_2 =$ _____

5. _____ law

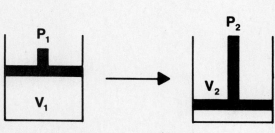

$P_1 = 3$
$V_1 = 90$

$P_2 = 9$
$V_2 =$ _____

3. _____ law

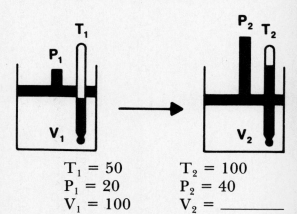

$T_1 = 50$
$P_1 = 20$
$V_1 = 100$

$T_2 = 100$
$P_2 = 40$
$V_2 =$ _____

6. _____ laws

Activity

Physical and Chemical Changes

The Ideal Gas Law

You have learned that a gas can be described according to three physical properties: temperature, volume, and pressure. Boyle's law states that an inverse variation exists between the volume and pressure of a gas. Charles's law states that a direct variation exists between the temperature and volume of a gas. Scientists have combined the laws of Boyle and Charles into one law called the ideal gas law. The equation for the ideal gas law is shown below:

$$PV = nRT$$

In this equation, P stands for pressure, V for volume, and T for temperature. The letter n represents the number of gas particles, and R is a constant. As you can see, the ideal gas law introduces a fourth variable in describing a gas: the number of particles. This is important, because changing the amount of a gas can have an effect on its pressure, volume, or temperature.

The ideal gas law is valuable because it shows how four physical properties of a gas are related. By studying this law, you can predict the behavior of a gas under a variety of circumstances. You can also explain why a gas behaves a certain way under certain conditions. Refer to the ideal gas law equation as you answer the following questions.

1. Two containers of the same size are filled with equal amounts of gas X. One container is rigid, while the other is flexible. Predict what will happen if each container is placed in an oven for 10 minutes. Give reasons for your answer.

   _____

   _____

   _____

   _____

   _____

   _____

2. A piston decreases the volume of a cylinder filled with gas Y. What will happen to the pressure of gas Y? Can you think of a way that the pressure could be held

   constant? _____

   _____

   _____

3. A metal container filled with gas Z is placed in ice. What will happen to the pressure of the gas? What will happen to the volume? Why? _____

_____

4. An infected tooth forms an abcess that fills with gas. The abcess puts pressure on the nerve of the tooth, causing a toothache. While waiting to see a dentist, the person with the toothache tries to relieve the pain by treating the infected area with moist heat. Will this treatment help? Why or why not? _____

_____

_____

5. Use the ideal gas law to explain each of the following situations:

a. A tire goes flat when a leak allows air to escape.

_____

_____

b. A balloon full of air shrinks when placed in a freezer.

_____

_____

c. A bottle of soda pop explodes when left out in the hot sun.

_____

_____

d. Bicycle tires seem higher in summer than in winter.

_____

_____

Laboratory Investigation

Chapter 2 ■ Physical and Chemical Changes

Observing a Candle

Problem
How can physical and chemical properties be distinguished?

Materials *(per group)*
small candle
matches
metric ruler
candle holder or small empty food can
sand

Procedure 🧪 👁 🔥 👉

1. On a separate sheet of paper, prepare a data table similar to the one shown here.

2. Observe the unlighted candle. List as many physical and chemical properties as you can.

3. Place the candle in the candle holder. If you are not using a candle holder, fill the small food can with sand and place the candle in the center of the sand. Make sure that the candle is placed securely.

4. Under your teacher's supervision, carefully light the candle.

5. Observe the lighted candle. Continue to list as many physical and chemical properties as you can. Record your observations in the correct columns in your data table.

	Physical properties	Chemical properties
Unlighted candle		
Lighted candle		

Observations

1. What physical properties of the unlit candle did you observe?

_____

_____

2. What senses did you use when you made these observations?

_____

3. What physical changes did you observe after you lit the candle?

_____

_____

4. What did you have to do to observe a chemical property of the candle?

_____

_____

5. What evidence of chemical change did you observe?

_____

_____

Analysis and Conclusions

1. What do you think is the basic difference between a physical property and a chemical property?

_____

_____

2. Can a physical property be observed without changing the substance?

_____

_____

3. What name is given to a process such as burning a candle? What is the result of such a process?

_____

_____

4. Which type of property—physical or chemical—is easier to determine? Why?

_____

_____

5. On Your Own Obtain a recipe for making bread. List the chemical and physical properties of the ingredients. How do the properties of the ingredients result in a loaf of bread?

_____

_____

Answer Key

Chapter Discovery: Observing Changes in Matter

Part A: 1. a. Answers will vary. b. Cube or rectangular prism c. White d. Sweet e. Brittle, solid but porous f. Crystalline, slightly rough surface   **3.** Crystals have been broken apart so that instead of a cube you now have many tiny pieces. It is still white and sweet and made of crystals.   **5.** The sugar may or may not be visible, depending on if all the sugar dissolved. Ideally students should use enough water so all the sugar dissolves; the sugar now is mixed with the water.   **6.** Yes, because the water tastes sweet.   **7.** Answers may vary. Some students may know that evaporating the water will reveal the sugar.   **Part B: 3.** In addition to the charring of the sugar in the bottom of the tube, students may be able to see water or water vapor on the sides of the test tube and smoke at the mouth; the actual chemical reaction taking place is the burning of the sugar to produce carbon, water, and carbon dioxide.   **5.** a. May not be much different from the size of the original sugar cubes b. Shapeless glob c. Black d. Tasteless or bitter; like charcoal e. Becomes hard as it cools f. Probably smooth   **6.** Color has changed from white to black; whole crystal structure seems to have broken down; remaining substance no longer tastes sweet. **7.** Answers may vary. The sugar actually is not present because it has changed into something else—the charred carbon in the bottom of the tube plus the water and carbon dioxide that formed as the sugar was burning.   **8.** In Part A, the sugar was still sugar; it just changed in form from solid to powder or from being separate to being mixed with water.   **9.** Answers may vary. Some students may realize that in a chemical change a substance actually changes into something else, while in a physical change the substances keeps its identity.

Chapter Activities
Discovery Activity: Observing a Phase Change

When the hot water vapor strikes the cooler glass, some of the water vapor condenses on the glass, giving it a cloudy look. Eventually drops of water form on the glass.

Activity: Properties of Matter

1. Chemical change   **2.** Physical change **3.** Physical change   **4.** Chemical change **5.** Melting, slow to fast   **6.** Vaporization, slow to fast   **7.** Evaporation, slow to fast **8.** Condensation, fast to slow

Discovery Activity: General and Specific Properties

Answers will vary depending on the substances students choose. Check that descriptions are reasonable.

Discovery Activity: Identifying Physical and Chemical Changes

Table A 1. Physical; phase change; no new compounds   **2.** Chemical; new compound is formed as gasoline is burned and carbon dioxide is produced   **3.** Physical; phase change; water evaporated leaving salt; change in physical appearance   **4.** Physical; no new product; sugar is merely dissolved, not changed chemically   **Table B** Possible answers: **1.** Break it. Spoils, producing sulfur smell.   **2.** Write with it; the graphite breaks off. Burned in trash, causing it to combine with oxygen and form carbon dioxide.   **3.** Pulverizing changes only its form. Dissolved in water, it produces carbon dioxide.   **4.** Breaking a stem rearranges its physical form. During growth the new plant produces new molecules from simple elements.   **5.** Bending it into a new shape;

melting it in scrap recycling plant. During rusting, iron and oxygen combine to form new compound, iron oxide.

Discovery Activity: Phase Changes

1. No (Increase in heat energy produces phase changes only.) **2.** Yes **3.** Yes **4.** Heat energy **5.** Particles (molecules) move further apart and also move faster. **6.** Phase changes occur at constant temperatures. Heat energy is either gained or lost during a phase change.

Discovery Activity: Pouring a Gas

2. Chemical change **3.** The flame goes out. Carbon dioxide, which is produced by the chemical reaction between vinegar and baking soda, does not support burning. This is a common test for carbon dioxide.

Problem-Solving Activity: Behavior of Gases

1. 50 Boyle's law **2.** 140 Charles's law **3.** 30 Boyle's law **4.** 30 Charles's law **5.** 30 Boyle's law **6.** 100 Boyle's and Charles's laws

Discovery Activity: The Ideal Gas Law

1. If temperature goes up, volume or pressure must also increase. Since the rigid container cannot change its volume, the pressure of the gas inside the container will increase. This may result in an explosion. Since the flexible container can change its volume, the gas inside this container will expand. The flexible container will probably become larger or look swollen. **2.** Pressure will increase. Pressure could be held constant if the gas were sufficiently cooled, or if some of the gas were removed. **3.** The pressure of the gas will decrease. The volume will stay the same because the metal container cannot change in size. **4.** No, because heat will only cause the gas to expand or the pressure to increase, both of which will increase the pressure on the nerve. A better pain reliever would be an ice pack, which would cause the abcess to shrink. **5.** a. As gas particles are removed, volume goes down. b. As temperature decreases, volume increases. c. As temperature increases, pressure increases. d. As temperature increases, pressure and volume increase.

Laboratory Investigation: Observing a Candle

Observations **1.** Mass, color, volume, shape, texture, hardness, odor. **2.** Touch, smell, sight, hearing. **3.** Wax became hotter and melted. **4.** Ignite the candle wick. **5.** New material (smoke) was produced.
Analysis and Conclusions **1.** Chemical properties can be detected only through interaction with other materials. **2.** Yes. **3.** Chemical change or chemical reaction. A new substance with new and different physical and chemical properties is formed. **4.** Physical, because observing physical properties of an object requires no other materials. **5.** Answers will vary depending on the recipe. In general, the mixing of the ingredients involves physical changes, and the baking of the bread involves chemical changes as well. If yeast is used as an ingredient, some chemical changes take place as the yeast rises before baking.

Contents

*Appropriate for cooperative learning

CHAPTER
Chapter Discovery   Mixtures, Elements, and Compounds 3

Types of Mixtures

Background Information

A mixture consists of two or more substances that are mixed together but not chemically combined. In this activity you will prepare some mixtures and observe their properties. You will also observe several common materials that are already in the form of a mixture.

Materials

8 clear glass jars with lids
3 small plates
teaspoon
sand
salt
sugar
cooking oil
vinegar
toothpaste
milk
mayonnaise
dry cereal
raisins
paint
jelly

Procedure

1. Fill a jar about three-fourths full with tap water. Add 1 teaspoonful of sand. Place a lid on the jar and shake the mixture vigorously.

2. Observe the mixture. Can you see clearly two or more substances? Record your observations in the Data Table.

3. Would you describe the mixture as clear, cloudy, or opaque? (Opaque means that no light can pass through a material.) Record your observation in the Data Table.

4. Is the mixture uniform throughout? That is, would a sample of the mixture taken from any part look just like any other sample? Write yes or no in the Data Table.

5. Suppose you wanted to separate the mixture into the substances that make it up. What method would you use? Write your idea in the Data Table. If you cannot think of a way to separate the substances, write "No idea."

6. Fill a second jar about three-fourths full with warm tap water. Add 1 teaspoonful of salt. Place a lid on the jar and shake the mixture vigorously.

7. Do steps 2 through 5 for this mixture.

8. Repeat steps 6 and 7 using sugar instead of salt.

9. Fill a jar about three-fourths full with water. Add several teaspoonfuls of cooking oil. Place a lid on the jar and shake the mixture vigorously. Do steps 2 through 5 for this mixture.

10. Repeat step 9 using vinegar instead of water.

11. Fill a jar about three-fourths full with dry cereal. Add a handful of raisins. Place a lid on the jar and shake the mixture vigorously. Do steps 2 through 5 for this mixture.

12. Pour some milk into a jar. Do steps 2 through 5 for milk, which is a mixture.

13. Repeat step 12 for paint.

14. Place a few spoonfuls of jelly on a small plate. Do steps 2 through 5 for jelly.

15. Repeat step 13 with mayonnaise; repeat step 13 again with toothpaste.

Observations

DATA TABLE

Mixture	Two or More Substances Visible?	Appearance	Uniform?	How Separate?
Sand/water				
Salt/water				
Sugar/water				
Oil/water				
Oil/vinegar				
Cereal/raisins				
Milk				
Paint				
Jelly				
Mayonnaise				
Toothpaste				

Critical Thinking and Application

1. Based on your observations, what are some ways in which mixtures differ from one another?

   _____

   _____

2. Which of the mixtures you tested would you say are the "best mixed"? Why?

   _____

   _____

   _____

3. Which of the mixtures you tested appear to be the "least mixed"? Why?

   _____

   _____

   _____

Activity

Classifying Matter

Use the terms listed below to complete the following diagram that illustrates the classification of matter.

Matter	Mixtures	Heterogeneous matter	Pure substances
Compounds	Elements	Solutions	Homogeneous matter

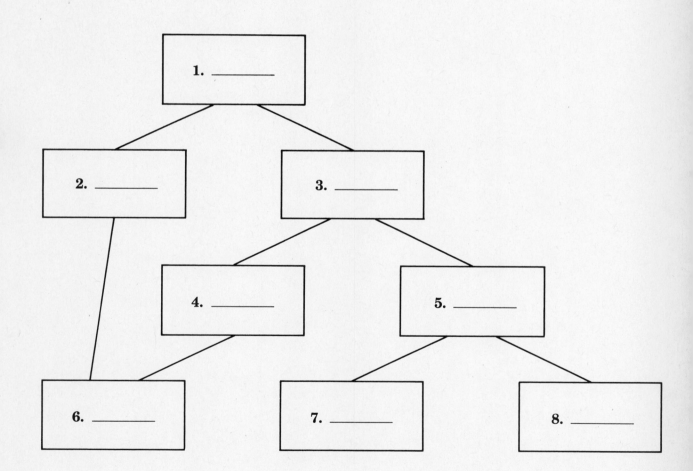

Activity

Mixtures, Elements, and Compounds

Separating Substances

1. On a sheet of paper, mix together a tablespoon of sand and an equal amount of salt. Observe the combined substances carefully. Record your observations in the Data Table.

2. Pour the combined substances into a glass of warm water. Stir. Record your observations in the Data Table.

3. Slowly pour the liquid into a pie tin or shallow dish. Carefully observe the remaining contents of the glass.

4. Place the pie tin or dish in sunlight for about 2 to 3 days. Record your observations in the Data Table.

DATA TABLE

Step	Observations
1	
2	
4	

Now answer the following questions.

1. Is the combination of salt and sand a mixture or a compound? Explain your answer.

   _____

   _____

   _____

2. Is the mixing of salt and sand a physical or a chemical change? What about the stirring of the combined substances in water?

   _____

   _____

   _____

3. What substance remains in the glass? How do you know?

_____

_____

_____

4. What happens to the water in the pie tin? What substance remains?

_____

_____

_____

5. How does this activity illustrate some properties of heterogeneous matter?

_____

_____

_____

_____

Activity   Mixtures, Elements, and Compounds

Counting Atoms

Calculate how many atoms of each element are present in the following compounds.

1. $NaHCO_3$

2. $C_2H_4O_2$

3. $Mg(OH)_2$

4. $3H_3PO_4$

5. $2H_2SO_4$

6. $(NH_4)_3PO_4$

7. $C_6H_{12}O_6$

8. $4CaCO_3$

Activity

CHAPTER
3

Elements, Compounds, Mixtures

1. Which of the following represent elements and which represent compounds?

    a. HC1   c. Na

    b. CO   d. Ca

2. Can two or more elements be combined chemically to make a new element? Explain your answer.

3. Do the relative proportions of elements in a given compound vary from sample to sample? Explain your answer.

4. Place the terms compounds, mixtures, and elements in the proper sequence according to increasing complexity.

_____ $\longrightarrow$ _____ $\longrightarrow$ _____

5. In the boxes below, diagram a heterogeneous and a homogeneous mixture. Use Xs to represent one kind of molecule and 0s to represent another kind.

Heterogeneous
mixture

Homogeneous
mixture

Activity

A Classification Scheme

The following table represents a way of classifying substances according to certain properties of matter. In the left column are several characteristics. Read across the table and determine if each type of matter given in the column head possesses that characteristic. Place a check in the appropriate box if it does.

Characteristic	Heterogeneous Mixture	Homogeneous Mixture	Solution	Compound
1. Does not settle out on standing				
2. Scatters light				
3. Can separate when allowed to stand				
4. Contains only fixed amounts of components				
5. Often appears cloudy				
6. Components do not lose their own properties				
7. Looks the same throughout				
8. Amounts of different components may vary				

Activity

Classifying Common Objects

1. Obtain samples of the following materials for observation: sugar, salt water, copper wire, taco shell, pencil eraser.

2. Use simple physical tests to determine which substances are mixtures, solutions, elements, or compounds.

3. Present your observations in the chart provided.

Substance	Classification	Properties
Sugar		
Salt water		
Copper wire		
Taco shell		
Pencil eraser		

Laboratory Investigation

Making Models of Chemical Reactions

Problem
How do atoms and molecules of elements and compounds combine in chemical reactions?

Materials *(per group)*
toothpicks
red, yellow, green, blue, purple (red-blue), and orange (yellow-red) food coloring
25 large marshmallows

Procedure
  A. *Making Marshmallow Atoms*
  1. Prepare model atoms by applying food coloring to the marshmallows as follows:
    N (nitrogen)—red (2)
    H (hydrogen)—blue (6)
    Cu (copper)—green (4)
    O (oxygen)—yellow (6)
    K (potassium)—orange (2)
    Cl (chlorine)—purple (2)

  2. Let the marshmallows dry for 2 hours.
  B. *Assembling the Marshmallow Molecules*
  1. Use a toothpick to join two red marshmallows to make a molecule of N_2. Use a toothpick to join two blue marshmallows to make a molecule of H_2.
  2. Ammonia (NH_3) is used in cleaning solutions and in the manufacture of fertilizers. A molecule of ammonia contains 1 nitrogen atom and 3 hydrogen atoms. Use the marshmallow molecules of nitrogen and hydrogen you made in step 1 to form an ammonia molecule. You may use as many nitrogen and hydrogen molecules as you need to make ammonia molecules as long as you do not have any atoms left over. Remember, hydrogen and nitrogen must start out as molecules consisting of 2 atoms each. Now balance the equation for the chemical reaction that produces ammonia:

$$\underline{\hspace{2cm}} N_2 + \underline{\hspace{2cm}} H_2 \rightarrow \underline{\hspace{2cm}} NH_3$$

  3. Use two green marshmallows for copper and one yellow marshmallow for oxygen to make a model of a copper oxide molecule (Cu_2O). With a white marshmallow representing carbon, manipulate the marshmallow models to illustrate the reaction below, which produces metallic copper. Balance the equation.

$$\underline{\hspace{2cm}} Cu_2O + \underline{\hspace{2cm}} C \rightarrow \underline{\hspace{2cm}} Cu + \underline{\hspace{2cm}} CO_2$$

Matter: Building Block of the Universe   N ■ 71

4. Use orange for potassium, purple for chlorine, and white for oxygen to assemble a molecule of potassium chlorate ($KClO_3$).

Observations

1. How many molecules of N_2 and H_2 are needed to produce 2 molecules of HN_3?

_____

2. How many molecules of copper are produced from 2 molecules of Cu_2O?

_____

Analysis and Conclusions

1. Which substances that you made are elements? Which are compounds?

_____

_____

2. If you had to make 5 molecules of ammonia (NH_3), how many red marshmallows would you need? How many blue marshmallows?

_____

_____

Answer Key

Chapter Discovery: Types of Mixtures

Check students' data tables for accuracy.
1. Answers may vary. Students should recognize such differences as appearance, ease of separation into components, consistency, and so forth. **2.** Answers may vary. Students may choose those mixtures in which separate substances cannot be seen, such as milk, or sugar and water. **3.** Answers may vary. Students may choose those mixtures in which two substances are clearly visible, such as cereal and raisins, or sand and water.

Activity: Classifying Matter

1. Matter **2.** Homogeneous matter
3. Heterogeneous matter **4.** Solutions
5. Pure substances **6.** Mixtures
7. Compounds **8.** Elements

Activity: Separating Substances

Observations Step 1: The sand and salt mixture appears tan and white. The separate particles of sand and salt can be observed. **Step 2:** The sand sinks to the bottom of the glass of warm water. The salt dissolves in the water. **Step 4:** After a few days the water evaporates. Salt remains in the pie tin or dish. **Questions 1.** The salt and sand combination is a mixture. The salt and sand did not combine chemically. Sand and salt were not present in a definite proportion.
2. Both are physical changes. **3.** Sand. It did not dissolve in the water; it remained in the glass when the salt water was poured out. **4.** The water evaporates. The salt remains. **5.** A heterogeneous mixture can be separated by physical means. The proportion of the substances that make up a heterogeneous mixture can vary.

Problem-Solving Activity: Counting Atoms

1. 1 sodium, 1 hydrogen, 1 carbon, 3 oxygen

2. 2 carbon, 4 hydrogen **3.** 1 magnesium, 2 oxygen, 2 hydrogen **4.** 9 hydrogen, 3 phosphorus, 12 oxygen **5.** 4 hydrogen, 2 sulfur, 8 oxygen **6.** 3 nitrogen, 12 hydrogen, 1 phosphorus, 4 oxygen **7.** 6 carbon, 12 hydrogen, 6 oxygen **8.** 4 calcium, 4 carbon, 12 oxygen

Activity: Elements, Compounds, Mixtures

1a. Compound **b.** Compound **c.** Element **d.** Element **2.** No, the chemical combination of elements produces compounds, not other elements. **3.** No, the elements in a given compound are always in fixed chemical proportions. **4.** Elements → compounds → mixtures **5.** Drawings will vary, but the Xs and Os should be evenly distributed in the homogeneous mixture and unevenly distributed in the heterogeneous mixture.

Activity: A Classification Scheme

1. Homogeneous mixture, solution, compound **2.** Heterogeneous mixture
3. Heterogeneous mixture **4.** Compound
5. Heterogeneous mixture **6.** Heterogeneous mixture, homogeneous mixture, solution
7. Homogeneous mixture, solution, compound **8.** Heterogeneous mixture, homogeneous mixture, solution. These categories represent very general statements. Depending on factors such as kind and size of particles and time allowed to stand, some of these categories would not have check marks and others would.

Discovery Activity: Classifying Common Objects

Sugar Compound, cannot be broken down easily by simple physical means **Salt water** Mixture, amounts of salt and water can vary **Copper wire** Element, cannot be broken down **Taco shell** Mixture, proportions of ingredients can vary **Pencil eraser** Compound, probably no longer made of natural rubber but of a mixture of several different chemical compounds

Laboratory Investigation: Making Models of Chemical Reactions

Observations **1.** 1 molecule of N_2, 3 molecules of H_2. **2.** 4. **Analysis and Conclusions** **1.** Elements are nitrogen, hydrogen, and copper. Compounds are NH_3, Cu_2O, CO_2, and $KClO_3$. **2.** 5 red and 15 blue.

Contents

CHAPTER 4

   (**Note:** *This investigation is found on page N102 of the student textbook.*)

*Appropriate for cooperative learning

Chapter Discovery | Atoms: Building Blocks of Matter | CHAPTER 4

Using Indirect Evidence

Background Information

   Indirect evidence is information that you gain about something without actually seeing it or touching it. In this activity you will use indirect evidence to prove that air is a form of matter. You will also use indirect evidence to describe some of the properties of air.

Materials

2 identical balloons, not inflated
marking pen
balance scale
tape measure
bucket or basin
freezer
oven

Procedure

1. Blow up one of the balloons and fasten it securely. Use the marking pen to label the balloon X.

2. Use the balance scale to determine the mass of the balloon that is not blown up.

   Record the mass here: _____

3. Examine balloon X and compare it to the balloon that is not blown up. How can you tell that there is something in balloon X?

   _____

4. Place balloon X on the balance scale and find its mass. Record the mass here: _____ How does the mass of balloon X compare with the mass of the balloon that is not blown up?

   _____

   _____

5. Fill a bucket or basin about three-quarters full with water. Place balloon X in the water. What happens? What can you tell about the density of the substance inside the balloon compared with the density of water?

   _____

6. Gently push against balloon X with your hands. How does the substance inside the balloon respond to the pressure of your hands?

_____

7. Hold balloon X near your ear and shake it. What can you tell about the substance inside the balloon?

_____

_____

_____

_____

8. Measure the circumference of balloon X with a tape measure. Record your

   measurement here: _____

9. Place balloon X in a freezer for about 20 minutes, then examine the balloon. Is there any evidence that the substance inside the balloon freezes at 0°C?

_____

   Measure the balloon with the tape measure. Record your measurement here: _____

   How does this measurement compare with the measurement that you made in step 8?

_____

10. Place balloon X in a warm oven for about 10 minutes. **CAUTION:** *Be very careful when lighting and using an oven. Only light an oven with adult supervision.*

11. Measure the balloon with the tape measure. Record your measurement here: _____
    What happened to the balloon?

_____

Critical Thinking and Application

12. You have learned in previous chapters that matter is anything that has mass and volume. What evidence do you have that air is matter?

_____

_____

_____

13. What can you conclude about the density of air? How do you know?

_____

_____

14. Based on your observations in step 6, would you describe air as rigid or flexible? Why?

_____

_____

15. Would you conclude from your observations that air is a solid, liquid, or gas? What evidence supports your conclusion?

_____

_____

_____

16. What happens to air when it is cooled? What happens when it is heated?

_____

17. Based only on the indirect evidence that you obtained in this activity, write a description of air.

_____

_____

_____

Name _____ Class _____ Date _____

Counting Atoms

The formula for a compound indicates the elements that make up the compound and the number of atoms of each element present in the compound. These numbers of atoms are indicated by the use of small numbers called subscripts. Sometimes groups of atoms act as a single atom. Such a group of atoms is called a polyatomic ion. If a polyatomic ion is used in a formula more than once, it is put in parentheses and the subscript appears outside the parentheses. When a subscript appears outside the parentheses, it indicates that all the elements inside the parentheses should be multiplied by that subscript. For example, the formula $Fe(OH)_3$ indicates the combination of 1 atom of iron, Fe, 3 atoms of oxygen, O, and 3 atoms of hydrogen, H.

In the following examples, list each element in the compound and the number of atoms of each element present. The first example has been done for you. You may already be familiar with some of the compounds.

Name	Use	Formula	Atoms in Formula
Calcium carbonate	Limestone	$CaCO_3$	Ca = calcium 1 C = carbon 1 O = oxygen 3
Aspirin	Pain reliever	$C_9H_8O_4$	
Magnesium hydroxide	Found in milk of magnesia	$Mg(OH)_2$	
Paradichlorobenzene	Moth crystals	$C_6H_4Cl_2$	
Acetic acid	Found in vinegar	$C_2H_4O_2$	
Trinitrotoluene (TNT)	Explosive	$C_7H_5(NO_2)_3$	
Calcium dihydrogen phosphate	Fertilizer	$Ca(H_2PO_4)_2$	

Name	Use	Formula	Atoms in Formula
Pyrite	Fool's gold	FeS_2	
Sucrose	Sugar	$C_{12}H_{22}O_{11}$	
Heptane	One of several components in gasoline	C_5H_{12}	
Sulfuric acid	Used in car batteries	H_2SO_4	
Cellulose	Found in wood products such as your pencil and paper	$C_6H_7O_2(OH)_3$	
Asbestos	Insulator	$H_4Mg_3Si_2O_9$	
Dichlorodiphenyl-trichloroethane (DDT)	Banned pesticide	$C_{14}H_9Cl_5$	
Silicon dioxide	Sand	SiO_2	
Iron oxide	Rust	Fe_2O_3	
Butane	Lighter fluid	C_4H_{10}	

Activity

Drawing Atoms

You can draw the structures of some common atoms by knowing their atomic number and number of neutrons. Using the information below, draw an atom of each substance. Remember to put the correct number of electrons in each energy level.

Substance	Atomic Number	Number of Neutrons
Helium	2	2
Lithium	3	4
Nitrogen	7	7
Fluorine	9	10
Neon	10	10

Activity

Atomic Structure

You can become more familiar with the atomic structure of some common substances by completing the chart below. For each substance, you have been given enough information to fill in all the blanks.

Substance	Symbol	Atomic Number	Mass Number	Number of Protons	Number of Neutrons	Number of Electrons
Helium	He	2	4			
Magnesium	Mg	12			12	
Zinc	Zn	30	65			
Bromine	Br		80			35
Aluminum	Al			13	14	
Uranium	U				146	92
Sodium	Na	11			12	
Krypton	Kr				48	36
Calcium	Ca		40	20		
Silver	Ag			47	61	

Activity

Making Models of Isotopes

Hydrogen has three isotopes: hydrogen-1, called protium; hydrogen-2, called deuterium; and hydrogen-3, called tritium. All have an atomic number of 1. Their mass numbers are 1, 2, and 3, respectively.

1. To represent the nuclei of these isotopes, draw a circle with a radius of 3 cm in the center of each of three sheets of paper. Using the same centers, draw a circle with a radius of 12 cm on each sheet to represent the area in which the electron is found. Label one diagram hydrogen-1, another hydrogen-2, and the third hydrogen-3. (Note that the diagrams are not drawn to scale.)

2. Using small circles of different colored paper to represent protons, electrons, and neutrons, indicate the number of each kind of particle in each atom by pinning or pasting the correct number of colored circles in the proper places.

3. In the space below, draw a diagram of each model of a hydrogen isotope you have constructed.

Protium

Deuterium

Tritium

Activity

Atoms: Building Blocks of Matter

Atomic Dimensions

The following examples are designed to help you become more familiar with the size of atoms, which are very, very small! By working through these examples, you may better understand how the parts of the atom are related to one another.

What Is the Size of One Atom?

1. It is estimated that about 1 trillion (1,000,000,000,000) atoms would fit into a period at the end of this sentence. If all the atoms were carbon atoms of the same size, and if the period had an approximate volume of 0.000,000,06 cubic centimeters, what would be the approximate size in cubic centimeters of just 1 atom? Now just think how many atoms it would take to make a colon!

2. If you inhaled 1000 cubic centimeters of air with one breath, about 200 cubic centimeters would be oxygen. The rest is mostly nitrogen. One molecule of oxygen is about 0.000,000,000,000,000,000,000,04 cubic centimeters in volume. About how many molecules of oxygen did you just inhale? This is not just a lot of hot air!

Space Inside the Atom

3. A nucleus occupies a very small amount of space inside an atom. From the nucleus to an electron is approximately 10,000 times the radius of the nucleus. Imagine the nucleus of an atom to be a ball 10 cm in diameter. How far away from this ball would the nearest hypothetical electron be? Could you throw the ball that distance so it reaches the electron?

Masses of Atoms

4. The atomic mass unit, amu, represents a very small amount of mass and is actually 0.000,000,000,000,000,000,000,001,67 g. Calculate your mass in grams, and then convert your mass to amu.

5. An electron is only 1/1836 the mass of a proton. If your mass was 50 kg, what would be the mass of something 1836 times smaller than you? Try it the other way. What would be the mass of something 1836 times larger than you?

Activity

Atoms: Building Blocks of Matter

Isotopes or Different Elements?

In each of the following statements, you are given a pair of elements and important information about each. Use this information to determine if the pair of elements are isotopes or different elements. Indicate your answer in the space provided.

1. Element D has 6 protons and 7 neutrons.
   Element F has 7 protons and 7 neutrons.

   _____

2. Element J has 27 protons and 32 neutrons.
   Element L has 27 protons and 33 neutrons.

   _____

3. Element X has 17 protons and 18 neutrons.
   Element Y has 18 protons and 17 neutrons.

   _____

4. Element Q has 56 protons and 81 neutrons.
   Element R has 56 protons and 82 neutrons.

   _____

5. Element T has an atomic number of 20 and
   an atomic mass of 40.
   Element Z has an atomic number of 20 and
   an atomic mass of 41.

   _____

6. Element W has 8 protons and 8 neutrons.
   Element V has 7 protons and 8 neutrons.

   _____

7. Element P has an atomic number of 92 and
   an atomic mass of 238.
   Element S has 92 protons and 143 neutrons.

   _____

Laboratory Investigation

Shoe Box Atoms

Problem
How can indirect evidence be used to build a model?

Materials *(per group)*
shoe box, numbered and taped shut, containing unidentified object(s)
balance
magnet

Procedure
1. Your teacher will give you a shoe box with an object or objects inside. Do not open or damage the box.
2. Use a magnet to determine if the objects in the box have any magnetic properties.
3. Determine the mass of an empty shoe box. Then determine the mass of your shoe box. The difference between the two masses is the mass of the object(s) inside your shoe box.
4. You may be able to determine something about the object's shape by tilting the box. Does the object slide? (flat) Does it roll? (rounded) Does it collide inside? (more than one object)
5. Shake the box up and down to determine if the object bounces. How hard does it bounce? Does it flip?
6. For each test you perform, record your observations in a data table similar to the one shown here.

Observations
1. How many objects are in your shoe box?

   _____

2. Is the object soft? Magnetic? Fragile?

   _____

3. Is the object flat, or rounded?

   _____

Test Performed	Results	
	Trial 1	Trial 2
Magnet brought near		
Mass of object(s) determined		
Box tilted		
Box shaken		

Analysis and Conclusions

1. Make a sketch of what you think is in the shoe box. Draw the object(s) to show relative size.

2. What other indirect evidence did you gather to help you make the drawing?

_____

_____

3. How does your sketch compare with the actual objects as reported by your teacher? Make a sketch of the actual contents of the box.

_____

_____

4. Describe how you can develop a model of an object without directly observing the object.

_____

_____

5. **On Your Own** Prepare a shoe box model with two items that you select. Have a classmate see if he or she can determine what is in your shoe box.

_____

_____

Answer Key

Chapter Discovery: Using Indirect Evidence

3. Balloon X is much bigger than the empty balloon. **4.** The mass of balloon X should be greater than the mass of the empty balloon. **5.** The balloon floats, so the density of the substances must be less than the density of water. **6.** It moves, but resists being compressed very much. **7.** Answers may vary. Some students may say "nothing," but this is not really true. You can tell that the substance does not rattle, roll, or splash; you can also conclude that it must fill the whole container. **9.** No, balloon X should shrink in the freezer. **11.** The balloon should expand in the oven. **12.** It must have volume, because it made the balloon get bigger. It must have mass, because balloon X had more mass than the empty balloon. **13.** The density of air is less than the density of water, because the balloon filled with air floated in water. **14.** Flexible, because the balloon could be pushed inward. **15.** Gas because its density is much less than that of water; it seems to fill the whole container in which it is placed; it is not hard or rigid; it does not seem to flow or splash. **16.** It contracts when cooled and expands when heated. **17.** Sample answer: Air is a form of matter. It is a gas. Its density is less than that of water. When cooled, air contracts. When heated, air expands.

Activity: Counting Atoms

$CaCO_3$ calcium 1, carbon 1, oxygen 3 $C_9H_8O_4$ carbon 9, hydrogen 8, oxygen 4 $Mg(OH)_2$ magnesium 1, oxygen 2, hydrogen 2 $C_6H_4Cl_2$ carbon 6, hydrogen 4, chlorine 2 $C_2H_4O_2$ carbon 2, hydrogen 4, oxygen 2 $C_7H_5(NO_2)_3$ carbon 7, hydrogen 5, nitrogen 3, oxygen 6 $Ca(H_2PO_4)_2$ calcium 1, hydrogen 4, phosphorus 2, oxygen 8 FeS_2 iron 1, sulfur 2 $C_{12}H_{22}O_{11}$ carbon 12, hydrogen 22, oxygen 11 C_5H_{12} carbon 5, hydrogen 12 H_2SO_4 hydrogen 2, sulfur 1, oxygen 4 $C_6H_7O_2(OH)_3$ carbon 6, hydrogen 10, oxygen 5 $H_4Mg_3Si_2O_9$ hydrogen 4, magnesium 3, silicon 2, oxygen 9 $C_{14}H_9Cl_5$ carbon 14, hydrogen 9, chlorine 5 SiO_2 silicon 1, oxygen 2 Fe_2O_3 iron 2, oxygen 3 C_4H_{10} carbon 4, hydrogen 10

Activity: Drawing Atoms

Check students' drawings for accuracy.

Problem-Solving Activity: Atomic Structure

Helium He 2 4 2 2 2   **Magnesium** Mg 12 24 12 12 12   **Zinc** Zn 30 65 30 35 30   **Bromine** Br 35 80 35 45 35   **Aluminum** Al 13 27 13 14 13   **Uranium** U 92 238 92 146 92   **Sodium** Na 11 23 11 12 11   **Krypton** Kr 36 83 36 48 36   **Calcium** Ca 20 40 20 20 20   **Silver** Ag 47 108 47 61 47

Activity: Making Models of Isotopes

Protium (hydrogen-1) contains one proton and no neutrons in the nucleus. **Deuterium** (hydrogen-2) contains one proton and one neutron in the nucleus. **Tritium** (hydrogen-3) contains one proton and two neutrons in the nucleus. All three isotopes of hydrogen contain one electron.

Problem-Solving Activity: Atomic Dimensions

Atomic Dimensions

1. $\dfrac{0.000,000,06 \text{ cm}^3}{1,000,000,000,000 \text{ atoms}} =$ 0.000,000,000,000,000,000,06 cm^3 per atom

2. $\dfrac{200 \text{cm}^3}{0.000,000,000,000,000,000,04 \text{ cm}^3 \text{ molecule}}$ = 5,000,000,000,000,000,000,000 molecules

3. $\dfrac{10 \text{ cm diameter}}{2}$ = 5 cm radius × 10,000 = 50,000 cm 50,000 cm = .5 km NO!

4. Assuming a mass of 45,400 grams:

$\dfrac{45,400 \text{ grams}}{0.000,000,000,000,000,000,000,001.67} =$ 27,100,000,000,000,000,000,000,000,000 amus

5. $50 \text{kg} \times \dfrac{1}{1836} = 0.027 \text{ kg}$

$50 \text{kg} \times 1836 = 91{,}800 \text{ kg}$

Problem-Solving Activity: Isotopes or Different Elements?

1. Different elements   **2.** Isotopes
3. Different elements   **4.** Isotopes
5. Isotopes   **6.** Different elements
7. Isotopes

Laboratory Investigation: Shoe Box Atoms

Observations   **1.–3.** All observations will depend on the items in the boxes. Observations should be checked to see if they are consistent with hidden items.   **Analysis and Conclusions**   **1.** Check student sketches to see if they are logical, based on observations. Students should not be graded on whether or not they were correct but on the scientific method employed.   **2.** Answers will vary but will likely include responses such as smell.   **3.** Students should be able to give valid reasons for any differences between their original sketch and the actual contents of the box.   **4.** Answers will vary but should be logical and demonstrate scientific method. **5.** Partners should be careful not to give any hints about the contents of their shoe boxes. Trade the boxes among the rest of your classmates.

Contents

*Appropriate for cooperative learning

Chapter Discovery   Classification of Elements: The Periodic Table

Chemical Pursuit

Background Information

Listed in Table 1 are 10 "mystery elements." By playing the game of Chemical Pursuit (which all good chemical detectives play), you can find clues about the properties of these elements. You can play the game alone, but you might enjoy finding a friend or family member to play it with you. You can either work on the mystery elements together, or compete to see who can collect the most clues in the fewest number of moves.

Materials

dice
paper clip or other small object
copy of board game from this activity

Procedure

1. Spread out the board game on a flat surface.

2. Place your paper clip or other small object on the box marked START. This object will be your marker as you play.

3. Roll one die. Read the number on the die and move your marker the same number of spaces.

4. Read the clue in the space on which you have landed. Note which mystery element it pertains to. Then copy the clue opposite that mystery element in Table 1.

5. Repeat steps 3 and 4.

6. Continue repeating steps 3 and 4 until you have moved your marker around the entire board game. When you pass START, continue around the game again. If you land on a clue that you have already copied, roll the die and move again.

7. Continue playing until you have collected at least three clues for each mystery element.

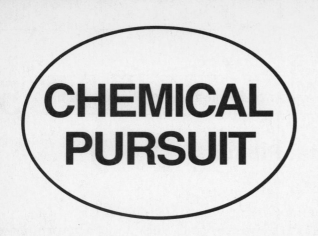

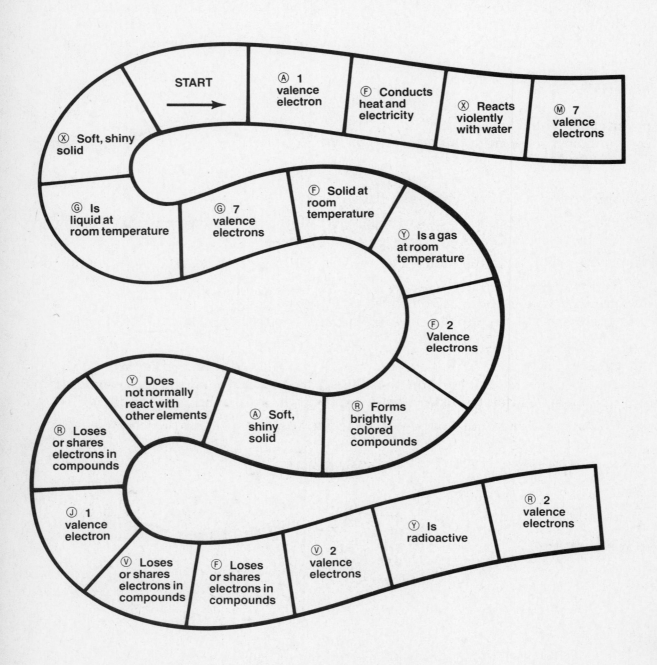

CHEMICAL PURSUIT

START

Ⓐ 1 valence electron

Ⓕ Conducts heat and electricity

Ⓧ Reacts violently with water

Ⓜ 7 valence electrons

Ⓧ Soft, shiny solid

Ⓖ Is liquid at room temperature

Ⓖ 7 valence electrons

Ⓕ Solid at room temperature

Ⓨ Is a gas at room temperature

Ⓕ 2 Valence electrons

Ⓨ Does not normally react with other elements

Ⓐ Soft, shiny solid

Ⓡ Forms brightly colored compounds

Ⓡ Loses or shares electrons in compounds

Ⓙ 1 valence electron

Ⓥ Loses or shares electrons in compounds

Ⓕ Loses or shares electrons in compounds

Ⓥ 2 valence electrons

Ⓨ Is radioactive

Ⓡ 2 valence electrons

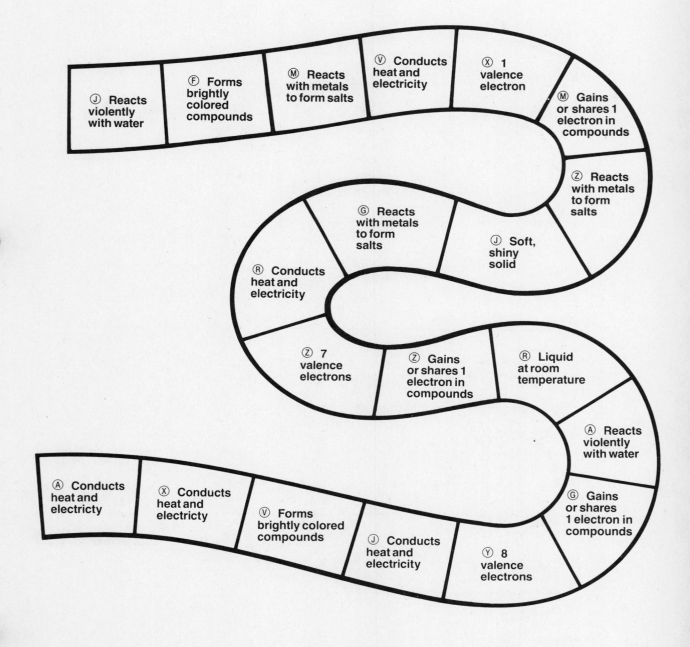

TABLE 1

Mystery Element	Clues
A	1. _____
	2. _____
	3. _____
F	1. _____
	2. _____
	3. _____
G	1. _____
	2. _____
	3. _____
J	1. _____
	2. _____
	3. _____
M	1. _____
	2. _____
	3. _____
R	1. _____
	2. _____
	3. _____
V	1. _____
	2. _____
	3. _____
X	1. _____
	2. _____
	3. _____

Mystery Element	Clues
Y	1. _____
	2. _____
	3. _____
Z	1. _____
	2. _____
	3. _____

Critical Thinking and Application

1. Look at the clues you have collected. Do some of the mystery elements seem like they belong together? Why?

_____

_____

_____

_____

_____

2. Suppose you wanted to classify the mystery elements in groups. What properties might you use to group the elements?

_____

_____

_____

_____

_____

3. Does one of the elements seem as if it should stand alone? If so, which one? What makes it different from the other elements?

_____

_____

_____

4. In the space below, make a chart in which you group the mystery elements in a way that makes sense to you. Write a sentence or two to explain why you grouped the elements as you did.

Activity

Classifying Objects

Mendeleev's table and the modern periodic table are systems of classifying the elements based on similar and different physical and chemical properties.

1. Choose a set of objects familiar to you, such as coins, stamps, marbles, leaves, playing cards, or jelly beans. Devise your own system of classifying the objects. Describe the basis for your system of classification.

_____

_____

_____

_____

_____

_____

_____

_____

2. In the space below, construct a data table for your results.

Activity   **Classification of Elements: The Periodic Table**

Metals and Nonmetals Around Home

See how many different metallic elements and nonmetallic elements you can find being used around your home. Remember, you are looking for elements. Materials like glass and plastic are not elements.

How many metals did you find? What are they? What nonmetals did you find? Complete the table below.

Metals	Nonmetals

What reasons can you give for the difference between the number of metals and the number of nonmetals you found?

_____

_____

_____

_____

_____

_____

_____

Activity

Heat Conductivity in Metals

1. Roll a piece of aluminum foil into a small cylinder about the size of a pencil.
2. Stand a metal teaspoon, iron nail, wooden strip, plastic spoon, and aluminum cylinder upright in a plastic cup.
3. Add hot water to the cup, leaving the tops of the objects above the water level.
4. Wait one minute. Carefully touch the exposed ends of each object in the cup.
5. Record your observations in the Data Table.

DATA TABLE

Material	How Good a Heat Conductor?	Ranking
Metal teaspoon		
Iron nail		
Wooden strip		
Plastic spoon		
Aluminum cylinder		

What materials are the best heat conductors?

_____

_____

_____

Activity   **Classification of Elements: The Periodic Table**

Halogens

Fluorine, chlorine, bromine, and iodine are halogens found in many household substances. Investigate their uses by looking for various substances in your home that contain these halogens. Make a chart of your findings. Include examples of the substances if possible.

Halogen	Household Substances	Uses
Fluorine		
Chlorine		
Bromine		
Iodine		

Activity   **Classification of Elements: The Periodic Table**

Element Code

Each numbered exercise contains element clues that will help you fill in the blanks and learn the identity of the missing word. Use the symbol for the element in each blank space.

1.
   a. Transition metal number 24   ___ ___ ___
   b. A common solid halogen   A baby's bed
   c. Family 13 bears this name

2.
   a. An active alkaline earth metal with 56 protons   ___ ___ ___
   b. The alkali metal of period 3   A delicious yellow fruit
   c. The metal element that makes up table salt

3.
   a. The first of the alkali metals   ___ ___ ___
   b. The first element of Family 16   The king of the jungle
   c. A period 2 nonmetal with 5 valence electrons

4.
   a. Element with atomic number 31   ___ ___ ___
   b. The last of the alkaline earth metals   A place to park the car
   c. Mendeleev predicted the existence of this metalloid

5.
   a. The first element in the actinoid series   ___ ___ ___
   b. Period 2 nonmetal with 6 valence electrons   A squirrel's treat
   c. The last of the noble gases

6.
   a. A transition metal used in incandescent light bulbs   ___ ___ ___ ___
   b. Period 4, Group 16 element   Watch out for a nest of these!
   c. The second element in Group 15
   d. Period 3 element with 6 valence electrons

Activity

Classification of Elements: The Periodic Table

Metal or Nonmetal?

1. Place samples of sulfur, charcoal, copper, and aluminum foil on a table or desk. Observe the luster of each.

2. Put on safety goggles. Place the samples on a wooden board and hammer each one. Observe the malleability of each.

3. Record your observations in the Data Table.

DATA TABLE

Sample	Luster	Malleability	Metal or Nonmetal?
Sulfur			
Charcoal			
Copper			
Aluminum foil			

Which samples are metals? Nonmetals?

_____

_____

_____

Activity — **Classification of Elements: The Periodic Table** — CHAPTER **5**

Identifying Substances

Complete the chart by first identifying each of the substances by name. Then describe each substance by placing a check in the appropriate box.

Substance	Name	Element	Compound	Symbol	Formula	Atom	Molecule
O							
O_2							
H							
H_2							
C							
CO							
Al							
NH_3							
Cl_2							
Au							
CO_2							
Ag							
Fe							
H_2O							
Hg							

Activity _____ CHAPTER

Classification of Elements: The Periodic Table 5

Identifying Unknown Elements

Use the periodic table on pages 114–115 of the textbook to identify the elements described in the statements below.

1. This element is in the same family as lead, and it has fewer protons than sodium.

_____

2. This element has an atomic number that is one greater than platinum.

_____

3. This element has the most protons of any element in Group 15.

_____

4. This element has more than 50 but less than 75 protons, and it is in Group 17.

_____

5. This Group 2 element has fewer protons than bromine, but more protons than sulfur.

_____

6. This element has the lowest atomic number of any Group 16 element.

_____

7. This element has an atomic number that is double the atomic number of silicon.

_____

8. This element has more valence electrons than oxygen, fewer valence electrons than neon, more protons than sodium, but fewer protons than argon.

_____

9. This element has an atomic number lower than that of aluminum and one less valence electron than the Group 16 elements.

_____

10. This element is in Group 1 and has a higher atomic number than chlorine, but a lower atomic number than bromine.

_____

Activity

Some Common Elements

1. Collect some samples of elements that are easily obtained, such as iron, copper, aluminum, nickel, and carbon. Make sure the elements you choose are safe to work with. On the lines below, indicate the elements you have collected and describe their properties.

_____

_____

_____

_____

_____

_____

_____

_____

_____

_____

2. Attach each element to a large square of paper. Make each square of paper look like a block on the periodic table.

3. On the square of paper, include the atomic number, atomic mass, name, and symbol of the element displayed.

4. In the space below, draw a diagram of each element square you have prepared. Be sure to include all the necessary information.

Activity   Classification of Elements: The Periodic Table   CHAPTER **5**

An Alien Periodic Table

In this activity you will place given physical and chemical properties of unknown elements in a blank periodic table.

Materials (*per student*)
blank periodic table, modified for this activity
list of observations on the unknown elements
pencil

Background Information

Earth's scientists have announced that they have made radio contact with intelligent life on a distant planet. One of this alien planet's languages has been translated, and scientific information has begun to be exchanged. The planet is composed of the same elements as Earth. However, the inhabitants of the planet have different names and symbols for them. Since the alien scientists do not know the names of our elements, they have radioed the following data on the known properties of the elements. Strangely, but luckily, there are no transition or rare earth elements on the alien planet. This means that their periodic table consists only of the "A" groups of elements. The data are as follows:

1. The inert gases are bombal (Bo), wobble (Wo), jeptum (J), and logon (L). Bombal (Bo) is a noble gas but does not have 8 valence electrons. The outside energy level of logon (L) is its second energy level. Of these noble gases, wobble (Wo) has the greatest atomic mass.

2. The alkali metals are xtalt (X), byyou (By), chow (Ch), and quackzil (Q). Of these alkali metals, chow (Ch) has the lowest atomic mass. Quackzil (Q) is in the same period as wobble (Wo).

3. The halogens are apstrom (A), vulcania (V), and kratt (Kt). Vulcania (V) is in the same period as quackzil (Q) and wobble (Wo).

4. The metalloids are ernst (E), highho (Hi), terriblum (T), and sississ (Ss). Sississ (Ss) is the metalloid with the highest atomic mass. Ernst (E) is the metalloid with the lowest atomic mass. Highho (Hi) and terriblum (T) are in Group 14. T has more protons than Hi. The element called yazzer (Yz) is a metalloid by location but has properties that suggest it is a light metal.

5. The most metallic element on the planet is called xtalt (X). The most chemically active nonmetal on the planet is called apstrom (A). The lightest element on the planet is called pfsst (Pf). The heaviest element on the planet is elrado (El). It is highly radioactive.

6. The chemical makeup of the alien planet's oceans seems to be about the same as Earth's oceans. When sea water is distilled, the liquid that is boiled off and then condensed has been shown to have molecules consisting of two atoms of pfsst (Pf) and one atom of nuutye (Nu). The solid left behind after the distillation consists mainly of a crystal made up of the elements byyou (By) and kratt (Kt).

7. The element called doggone (D) has only 4 protons in its atom.

8. Floxxit (Fx) is a black crystal and has 4 electrons in its outermost energy level. Both rhaatrap (R) and doadeer (Do) have atoms with four energy levels. But rhaatrap is less metallic than doadeer.

9. Magnificon (M), goldy (G), and sississ (Ss) are all members of Group 15. Goldy has fewer total electrons than magnificon.

10. Urrp (Up), oz (Oz), and nuutye (Nu) all gain 2 electrons. Nuutye is diatomic. Oz has a lower atomic number than urrp.

11. The element anatom (An) tends to lose 3 electrons. The elements zapper (Z) and pie (Pi) both lose 2 electrons. Pie loses them from its fifth energy level, while zapper loses them from its third.

Procedure

Fill in the blank periodic table below with the correct alien planet symbol for each element. The symbol is given in parentheses after the element name in the data statements.

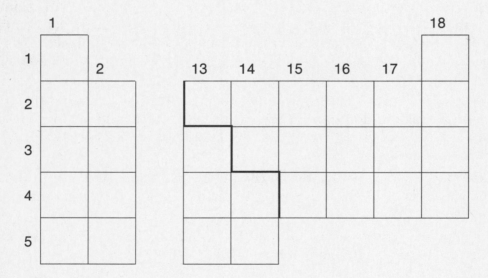

Activity

Interpreting the Periodic Table

Examine the hypothetical periodic table shown below. Use this periodic table to answer the questions that follow.

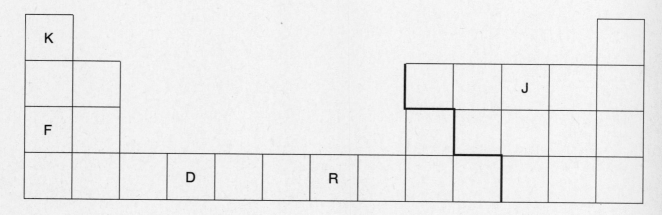

1. Which pair of elements has the same number of valence electrons?

   _____

2. Which pair of elements is in the same period?

   _____

3. Which pair of elements is in the same family?

   _____

4. Which element has the smallest atomic number?

   _____

5. Which elements would be classified as metals?

   _____

6. If the atomic number of Element D is 20, then what is the atomic number of element R?

   _____

Activity

Classification of Elements: The Periodic Table

Valence Clues

The diagrams below represent various atoms in which only the valence electrons are shown. Use the diagrams to provide the missing information.

	Element	Number of Valence Electrons	Metal, Nonmetal, Metalloid, Noble Gas	Group Number	Period Number
1.	_____	_____	_____	_____	_____
2.	_____	_____	_____	_____	_____
3.	_____	_____	_____	_____	_____
4.	_____	_____	_____	_____	_____
5.	_____	_____	_____	_____	_____

6.  _____ _____ _____ _____ _____

7.  _____ _____ _____ _____ _____

8.  _____ _____ _____ _____ _____

Activity   Classification of Elements: The Periodic Table

Element Maze

Read the statement in each box. Decide whether it is true or false. Move to the next box by following the arrow that corresponds to your answer. Continue your moves until you reach the end of the maze.

Start

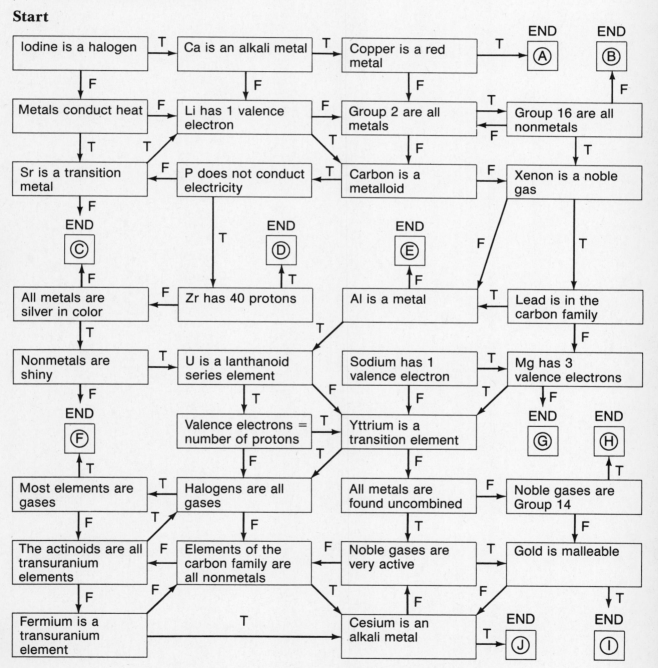

_____ *Laboratory Investigation* _____

CHAPTER 5 ■ Classification of Elements: The Periodic Table

Flame Tests

Problem
How can elements be identified by using a flame test?

Materials *(per group)*
nichrome or platinum wire
cork
Bunsen burner
hydrochloric acid (dilute)
distilled water
8 test tubes
test tube rack
8 chloride test solutions
safety goggles

Procedure 🧪 🔥 🧤 ☒ 👁

1. Label each of the test tubes with one of the following compounds: $LiCl$, $CaCl_2$ KCl, $CuCl_2$ $SrCl_2$, $NaCl$, $BaCl_2$, unknown.

2. Pour 5 mL of each test solution in the correctly labeled test tube. Be sure to put the correct solution in each labeled test tube.

3. Push one end of a piece of nichrome or platinum wire into a cork. Then bend the other end of the wire into a tiny loop.

4. Put on your safety goggles. Clean the wire by dipping it into the dilute hydrochloric acid and then into the distilled water. You must clean the wire after you make each test. Holding the cork, heat the wire in the blue flame on the Bunsen burner until the wire glows and no longer colors the burner flame.

5. Dip the clean wire into the first test solution. Hold the wire at the tip of the inner cone of the burner flame. Record the color given to the flame in a data table similar to the one shown here.

6. Clean the wire by repeating step 4.

7. Repeat step 5 for the other six known test solutions. Remember to clean the wire after you test each solution.

8. Obtain an unknown solution from your teacher. After you clean the wire, repeat the flame test for this compound.

Compound	Color of Flame
Lithium chloride	
Calcium chloride	

Observations

1. What flame colors are produced by each compound?

2. What flame color is produced by the unknown compound?

Analysis and Conclusions

1. Is the flame test a test for the metal or for the chloride in each compound? Explain your answer.

   _____

   _____

2. Why is it necessary to clean the wire before you test each solution?

   _____

   _____

3. What metal is present in the unknown solution? How do you know?

   _____

   _____

4. How can you use a flame test to identify a metal?

   _____

   _____

5. What do you think would happen if the unknown substance contained a mixture of two compounds? Could each metal be identified?

   _____

   _____

6. **On Your Own** Suppose you are working in a police crime laboratory and are trying to identify a poison that was used in a crime. How could a knowledge of flame tests help you?

   _____

   _____

   _____

Answer Key

Chapter Discovery: Chemical Pursuit

1. Answers may vary. Students should recognize that several of the elements have similar properties, such as the number of valence electrons or the ability to conduct heat and electricity.   **2.** Possible answers: number of valence electrons, phase at room temperature, ability to conduct heat and electricity, behavior in forming compounds, and reactions with other substances.
3. Element Y is modeled after the radioactive noble gas radon. Students may note such properties as 8 valence electrons, radioactive, and does not react with other elements.
4. Accept all reasonable answers. Mystery elements A, J, and X are modeled after the alkali metals; elements F, R, and V are modeled after the transition metals, and R is specifically modeled after mercury; elements G, M, and Z are modeled after the halogens, and G is modeled specifically after bromine. Students may or may not see these groupings, however. At this time, do not correct them, but simply allow them to get a feel for the types of properties that are similar among groups of elements.

Discovery Activity: Classifying Objects

Answers will vary depending on the objects students select. Accept all classification systems that seem logical.

Discovery Activity: Metals and Nonmetals Around Home

Answers will vary. Students may have problems finding pure metals and nonmetals in their homes because of the extensive use of synthetic materials. Examples of metals are copper in electrical wiring, silver in silverware, iron in nails, aluminum in cooking utensils. Examples of nonmetals are carbon in charcoal and diamonds and iodine in antiseptics. Students will probably find more metals than nonmetals, since most elements are metallic.

Also many metallic elements are useful because of their high melting point, malleability, and ductility.

Discovery Activity: Heat Conductivity in Metals

Answers will vary depending on the materials students select. However, students should observe that metals conduct heat better than nonmetals. Accept all reasonable rankings, as it might be hard for some students to discern subtle differences in heat conduction.

Activity: Halogens

Fluorine toothpaste, mouthwash, drinking water; prevents tooth decay   **Chlorine** bleach, cleansers; whitens clothing, germicide   **Bromine** food additives; whitens flour, kills pests   **Iodine** iodine solution; antiseptic

Problem-Solving Activity: Element Code

1. Cr l B   **2.** Ba Na Na   **3.** Li O N   **4.** Ga Ra Ge   **5.** Ac O Rn   **6.** W As P S

Discovery Activity: Metal or Nonmetal?

Sulfur dull, not malleable, nonmetal
Charcoal dull, not malleable, nonmetal
Copper shiny, malleable, metal **Aluminum foil** shiny, malleable, metal

Activity: Identifying Substances

Check students' charts for accuracy.

Activity: Identifying Unknown Elements

1. Carbon   **2.** Gold   **3.** Bismuth   **4.** Iodine   **5.** Calcium   **6.** Oxygen   **7.** Nickel   **8.** Chlorine   **9.** Nitrogen   **10.** Potassium

Activity: Some Common Elements

Answers will vary depending on the elements

students select. Check to make sure that the samples selected are elements. Check answers against a periodic table.

Problem-Solving Activity: An Alien Periodic Table

The answers listed include the data statements used as well as the element symbol. **1** Pf(5, 6) Ch(2, 6) By(2, 6) Q(2) X(2, 5) **2** D(7) Z(11) Do(8) Pi(11) **13** E(4) Yz(4) R(8) An(11) **14** Fx(8) Hi(4) T(4) El(5) **15** G(9) M(9) Ss(4, 9) **16** Nu(6, 10) Oz(10) Up(10) **17** A(3, 5) Kt(1, 3, 6) V (3) **18** Bo(1) L(1) J(1) Wo(1)

Problem-Solving Activity: Interpreting the Periodic Table

1. K and F **2.** D and R **3.** K and F **4.** K **5.** K, D, F, and R **6.** 23

Problem-Solving Activity: Valence Clues

1. sodium 1 metal 1 3 **2.** magnesium 2 metal 2 3 **3.** aluminum 3 metalloid 13 3 **4.** silicon 4 metalloid 14 3 **5.** phosphorus 5 nonmetal 15 3 **6.** sulfur 6 nonmetal 16 3 **7.** chlorine 7 nonmetal 17 3 **8.** argon 8 noble gas 18 3

Problem-Solving Activity: Element Maze

The correct route through the maze is **Iodine is a halogen** to **Ca** to **Li** to **Carbon** to **Xenon** to **Lead** to **Al** to **U** to **Yttrium** to **Halogens** to **Elements of the carbon family** to **The actinoids** to **Fermium** to **Cesium** to end.

Laboratory Investigation: Flame Tests

Observations 1. LiCl: crimson; $CaCl_2$: yellow-red; KCl: violet; $CuCl_2$: blue-green; $SrCl_2$: red; NaCl: yellow; $BaCl_2$: green-yellow. **2.** Answers will depend on your choice of the unknown chloride. **Analysis and Conclusions 1.** The metal, because each compound contained a chloride. If the test showed the presence of chlorine, the color would be the same in all the tests. **2.** To remove any substances from prior flame tests that might provide a false color. **3.** Answers will vary depending on the unknown chloride chosen. **4.** By its characteristic color. **5.** The color would be a mixture of the colors produced by each metal. No. You could not identify the two metals by a flame test alone. **6.** Flame tests, as well as other chemical procedures, can be used to identify the presence of poisonous elements in food or on clothing.

Science Reading Skills

TO THE TEACHER

One of the primary goals of the *Prentice Hall Science* program is to help students acquire skills that will improve their level of achievement in science. Increasing awareness of the thinking processes associated with communicating ideas and reading content materials for maximum understanding are two skills students need in order to handle a more demanding science curriculum. Teaching reading skills to junior high school students at successive grade levels will help ensure the mastery of science objectives. A review of teaching patterns in secondary science courses shows a new emphasis on developing concept skills rather than on accumulating factual information. The material presented in this section of the Activity Book serves as a vehicle for the simultaneous teaching of science reading skills and science content.

The activities in this section are designed to help students develop specific science reading skills. The skills are organized into three general areas: comprehension skills, study skills, and vocabulary skills. The Science Gazette at the end of the textbook provides the content material for learning and practicing these reading skills. Each Science Gazette article has at least one corresponding science reading skill exercise.

Contents

Shirley Ann Jackson: Helping Others Through Science
Science Reading Skill: Making Inferences

An inference is a reasonable conclusion based on evidence. For example, if you see dark rain clouds in the sky, you make the inference that it is going to rain. Much of the reading you do requires that you make inferences and arrive at certain conclusions by "reading between the lines." This means that you need to think while you are reading. You need to use the evidence provided to reach a reasonable conclusion. The conclusion is not stated outright. The ability to use this skill will make reading material more interesting and help you to understand how scientists think and reason while solving problems.

Practice the skill of making inferences by answering the questions below. Write your answers in complete sentences on the lines provided.

1. How might understanding the universe as it was in the past help us to understand it as it is now and as it will be in the future?

_____

_____

_____

_____

_____

2. What are Dr. Jackson's two main areas of scientific research? Which one relates more directly to everyday life?

_____

_____

_____

_____

_____

3. How could this area of research improve our everyday lives?

_____

_____

_____

_____

Science Reading Skill: Understanding Prefixes

A prefix is a group of letters that can be added to the beginning of a word. A prefix can have a meaning that affects the overall meaning of the word with which it is combined.

Look at the following list of prefixes and their meanings. By drawing lines, connect each prefix with a word on the right to form a new word that appears in this article. Then write each word and its meaning expressed in your own words on the lines provided.

1. **sub**   under the category of; part of   vision
2. **electro**   indicating electric   act
3. **inter**   with or on each other   atomic
4. **semi**   partly, not fully   conductor
5. **tele**   from a distance   magnetic

6. _____

_____

_____

7. _____

_____

_____

8. _____

_____

_____

9. _____

_____

_____

10. _____

_____

_____

Acid Rain: It Won't Go Away
Science Reading Skill: Skimming for Information

Skimming is a valuable skill for getting a particular piece of information quickly. You skim when you look for a word in the dictionary, when you use a telephone directory, or when you read a timetable looking for a train that will get you to the city before noon. In each case, you are looking for one particular item, and your eyes disregard everything else.

When you need to find a specific answer to a question in your text, it is not necessary to reread the entire chapter. Instead, let your eyes pass quickly over the reading material while you try to find key words, or the most important words, in the question. Then look for such clues as a number, a capital letter, a date, an italicized or boldfaced word, or quotation marks.

Working with this article, practice your skill in skimming. All of the questions in the following exercise are factual. You should be able to find the answers quickly and accurately. Wherever possible, use the clues discussed above. Write your answers on the lines provided.

1. According to an environmental official from Pennsylvania, what caused the acid rain that fell in parts of his state?

_____

2. Name the two types of chemical pollutants that make up acid rain.

_____

3. About how many miles of streams across the United States may be in danger of being poisoned from acid rain?

_____

4. What company employs F. D. Bess?

_____

5. How can the installation of "scrubbers" in smokestacks help reduce the amount of chemical pollutants being released into the air?

_____

6. About how many trout ponds and lakes in the Adirondacks no longer support fish?

_____

7. In what year did William B. Middendorf speak to Congress about acid rain?

_____

8. What is considered to be one of the chief sources of acid rain in the Northeast?

_____

9. How can acid rain affect such things as bricks, concrete, and statues made of stone?

_____

10. Why may it be difficult to compare the acidity of rain today with the acidity of rain in the 1950s?

_____

_____

Science Reading Skill: Critical Reading

Critical reading is careful, thoughtful reading. Some of the important skills involved are examining and evaluating the facts, making inferences, and understanding word meanings from context.

A critical reader examines the facts given in the article to see how they relate to the topic of the article. Seeing this relationship helps the reader to understand the author's main point. In evaluating the facts, the reader compares them to what he or she already knows. An inference is based on a suggestion the author makes, an idea not directly stated in the reading material. When the reader makes an inference, he or she comes to a reasonable conclusion based on information stated in the article. A critical reader tries to understand the meaning of an unfamiliar word from the way it is used in the context of a sentence or paragraph and from other familiar words surrounding it. Most importantly, a reader should think along with the author while reading.

Reread the article carefully and thoughtfully. Then answer the following questions. Where indicated, circle the letter of your choice or write your answers on the lines provided.

1. One source of acid rain can be traced to

   a. national wildlife.

   b. Colorado Springs.

   c. Canada.

   d. Adirondack lakes.

2. In the first paragraph under the subtopic "Is There a Solution?," the word that means to make something ineffective is

_____

3. The main point of this article is that

   a. the problem of acid rain is becoming increasingly menacing to our environment.

   b. the problem of acid rain is greatly exaggerated by conservationists.

   c. acid rain can be traced to the northwestern part of the United States.

   d. acid rain is actually pure rain that is slightly acidic.

4. How do you think acid rain can get into our drinking water?

_____

5. a. Name two artificial sources of pollutants that enter our atmosphere.

_____

b. Name two natural sources of pollutants that enter our atmosphere.

_____

6. While the author does not state it, the article suggests that
   a. industry use low-sulfur coal.
   b. Canadians blame American industries for polluting their lakes.
   c. more research is needed to solve the acid rain problem.
   d. the cause of acid rain is from chemicals in sewage.

7. Find the subtopic "How Bad Is It?" In the last sentence, what does the word "culprit" describe?

_____

8. What could happen to a metal object exposed to acid rain over a long period of time?

_____

Factories Beyond Earth
Science Reading Skill: Drawing Conclusions

In solving a crime, a good detective investigates the facts and follows any clues. With a little luck and a lot of careful reasoning, the detective draws conclusions that crack the case.

When reading science material, you must act as a detective. Gather all the information that relates to the topic. Be alert to ideas the author seems to suggest, which are not on the printed page. Then, after carefully evaluating all the evidence, you will be ready to draw reasonable conclusions.

In the last paragraph of this article, the author raises some interesting and challenging questions about manufacturing processes in space. Given all the facts and ideas in the article, draw your own conclusions and answer the questions below. Write your answers in complete sentences on the lines provided.

1. Why do you think it would be important for steel to be acid-resistant if it is going to be shipped to Earth?

   _____

   _____

2. Is there a valid reason to conclude that kidney cells produce more of a special chemical when they are grown in space rather than on Earth? Explain.

   _____

   _____

3. How do you think pure products manufactured in orbiting factories could reach the consumer on Earth without being contaminated?

   _____

   _____

4. a. If you were a manufacturer in space, what would you manufacture that would be useful to people on Earth?

   _____

   _____

   b. Could you manufacture this product more efficiently in space than on Earth? Explain.

   _____

   _____

Science Reading Skill: Making Inferences

An inference is a reasonable guess based on evidence and on your own past experience. You make inferences in a variety of situations in your daily life. For instance, when you see dark clouds hanging low in the sky, you infer that it is going to rain. And although your friend does not tell you, you infer that she is bitterly disappointed about not getting the lead in the show. You make this inference from watching her eyes fill with tears and her lips tremble.

Much of the reading you do requires that you make inferences by "reading between the lines." Authors do not always tell you everything because they expect you to discover some things for yourself. You can infer the meaning of a new word by using other familiar words in the sentence or paragraph as clues. Making inferences can help you to understand the author's ideas, including those that are only suggested and not printed in the text.

The ability to use inference skills should make reading more interesting. It should also help you to understand how scientists think and reason when solving problems.

Reread the article carefully. You will need to make inferences to answer the following questions. Write your answers on the lines provided.

1. Find the word "molten" in the first paragraph. a. Write your definition. b. List the clues, other words, or phrases that helped you define "molten."

   a. Definition: _____

   b. Clues: _____

   _____

2. Refer to the first paragraph. a. What was the level of gravity? b. How can you tell? What were the clues?

   a. Level of gravity: _____

   b. Clues: _____

   _____

3. Look at the illustration on the last page of the article. Read the caption. What important condition exists both in space and underwater?

   _____

4. Find the subtopic "Space Metals."

   a. Do you think the author suggests that travel between space and Earth will be popular?

   _____ Yes _____ No

   b. How do you know?

   _____

   _____

   _____

Shirley Ann Jackson: Helping Others Through Science

Making Inferences possible answers:
1. Understanding how the universe was formed can help scientists understand how atoms and their components interact and the nature of matter. This insight still applies today and would apply in the future. **2.** She is studying the nature of matter, which involves experimenting with subatomic particles. She is also studying semiconductors and optoelectronic materials. Semiconductors and optoelectronics are probably more closely related to our everyday lives. **3.** It could improve communications and the quality of computers and television. **Understanding Prefixes 1.** subatomic **2.** magnetic **3.** act **4.** conductor **5.** vision Possible answers: **6.** Having to do with parts of atoms **7.** Exhibiting the properties of electricity and magnetism **8.** To act on each other **9.** Something that conducts electricity to some degree but not as fully as a metal **10.** Device that receives and projects a picture over a distance

Acid Rain: It Won't Go Away

Skimming for Information 1. Pollutants from the Midwest **2.** Sulfur dioxide and oxides of nitrogen **3.** 100,000 **4.** Union Carbide Corporation **5.** Scrubbers clean emissions before they rise into the air. **6.** 180 **7.** 1980 **8.** Industries in the Ohio Valley **9.** Wears them down; erodes them **10.** Earlier measurements may have been wrong. **Critical Reading 1.** c **2.** Neutralize **3.** a **4.** From reservoirs **5.** a. Automobile engines and industrial factories b. volcanoes, forest fires **6.** c **7.** Factories **8.** It could turn green.

Factories Beyond Earth

Drawing Conclusions 1. Pollutants in the atmosphere on Earth would erode the steel. **2.** Yes, an experiment performed in space in 1975 proved to be true. **3.** Accept reasonable answers. **4.** Student answers will vary. **Making Inferences 1a.** melted by heat; b. sun's intense rays; temperature of iron rose; began to melt **2a.** Zero **b.** Iron hanging in space; astronauts floating **3.** Weightlessness **4.** The author states that some of these metals would be used as thin, protective coatings on everything from Space Shuttles to Earthbound craft.